MUSEUMS & GALLERIES
COMMISSION

1992
Prayer or Promise?

The opportunities for
Britain's museums and the people
who work in them

Kenneth Hudson

LONDON: HMSO

© Crown copyright 1990

First published 1990

ISBN 0 11 290504 8

British Library Cataloguing in Publication Data

A CIP catalogue record for this book is
available from the British Library

1992

1992 is a shorthand expression, used to describe the following situation.

At a summit meeting held in Luxembourg in 1985, the member states of the European Community signed the Single European Act. This was and still is a declaration of intentions, the implementation of which is partly a matter of interpretation, and therefore of potential disagreement, partly of practicability – and there is bound to be argument as to whether this or that measure is practicable or not – and partly of circumstances, which may be very different on 31st December 1992, when the Act is due to come into operation.

Foreword

by the Chairman of the Museums & Galleries Commission,
Lord Morris of Castle Morris

We have in the past two or three years been encouraged from every direction to take up crystal ball-gazing. What will that magic date bring, riches or regrets? In Mr Hudson's phrase, a Prayer or a promise? We can I believe be sure only that 1992 will bring change to our lives, although, as often in life, the reality will quite likely match neither our greatest hopes nor our worst fears, but rather gently settle somewhere in between.

The Museums & Galleries Commission intends to play its own part in ensuring that the interests of our constituents – museums and galleries throughout the United Kingdom, and the people who work in them – are protected and furthered in the greater Europe which is taking shape around us. It has long seemed to us that one of the greatest needs at the present time is for simple, hard facts to emerge from the welter of speculation and wishful thinking. It is gratifying to see that Kenneth Hudson in this study reaches much the same conclusion.

This report has been commissioned as a contribution to the European debate. It does not answer all the questions, nor does it necessarily represent the views of the Museums & Galleries Commission. And nor should it. Kenneth Hudson is an internationally known observer of the museum scene, whose reputation in Europe and beyond is entirely justified by his truly encyclopaedic knowledge of museums. He is a forthright individualist, someone who remains unperturbed by the vagaries of fashion. And he is an excellent companion to guide us through the murky uncharted waters of the Europe to come.

We live in interesting times. As Mr Hudson points out, 1989, not 1992, may turn out to be the crucial year for Europe. Events in Eastern Europe could hasten, slow or render unnecessary the whole process of '1992'. As this report is published, one can I believe feel optimistic that we might, for the first time in fifty years, be within sight of a new golden age when we can all as equals partake of our great European cultural heritage. And that is a consummation devoutly to be wished, and towards which we all should strive.

MORRIS

Preface

It should be made clear that, although I have had numerous helpful conversations with members of the staff of the Commission during the preparation of this Report, the opinions eventually expressed in it are entirely my own and the Commission has no responsibility for them, although I have always been careful to respect their views.

My research would not have been possible without the co-operation of many well-informed people throughout Western Europe. They will, I am sure, be relieved to find that their frank and not infrequently heretical contributions to the discussions remain anonymous. I have constantly been impressed by the unreality of such generalisations as 'The feeling in the French museums world seems to be', or 'Dutch museums are worried about the erosion in the value of their annual grants'. There are unfashionable, courageous and out-of-date opinions to be found in every country, and one gradually learns to distinguish between those which represent the beginnings of a trend and those which have had their day.

One gradually acquires the art, too, of realising when the present tense should really be the future. Many official pronouncements are worded in a manner which suggests that a decision has actually been taken and that activity is in progress, whereas a more practised and more cynical approach may well lead to the conclusion that what one is really faced with is wishful thinking, often on a major scale. There is quite a lot about the European Community which is utopian, and most unlikely ever to happen at all. Those who are unable to see this may well find themselves building their plans on sand.

The line between faith and fantasy is, of course, difficult to draw. Optimism is usually a virtue and one earns no gratitude by being perpetually depressing. On the other hand, however, it is both irresponsible and cruel to encourage false hopes. In the pages which follow I have tried to steer what seems to me a reasonable course between the extreme of day-dreaming and disbelief and, above all, to produce recommendations which stand some chance of success.

I hold no permanent public position, either in Britain or on the Continent, and I should therefore be well-placed to deliver objective judgements. My working base is in England, but I spend so much time out of my native country that I feel no temptation whatever to take up chauvinistic attitudes. I think I can truthfully say that I am not a typical Englishman – I am disqualified from this by speaking several languages – and, equally, that I feel European. I hope this standpoint emerges from what follows.

Introduction
The European museum situation in 1990

Within the countries of Western Europe – the Council of Europe's Europe – there are at the present time about 16,000 museums, of which all but 2,500 are in the territory of the member states of the European Community. These figures have to be interpreted with care, partly because the total is growing by about one per cent each year and partly because the sources of information are unreliable. Many village museums, private museums and museums belonging to industrial and commercial undertakings do not find their way into the official lists, which tend to be somewhat snobbish and conservative in these matters. There could well be as many as 2,000 museums of this kind, but it seemed prudent to omit the possibility from our present calculations.

Crude totals and percentages do, of course, present a somewhat misleading picture of Europe's museum world. They offer few clues to the size or quality of the museums concerned, to the balance between one type of museum and another, or to the proportion of museums in any particular country which are financed and run by foundations or associations, as distinct from national or local government. But they do, even so, tell us a few things of value. They allow us, for instance, to identify those countries which have a great many museums and those with relatively few. There are three divisions.

Countries with more than 1,500 museums
France, the Federal Republic of Germany, Great Britain, Italy.

Countries with between 500 and 1,500 museums
Austria, Belgium, Finland, the Netherlands, Spain, Switzerland.

Countries with fewer than 500 museums
Denmark, Greece, the Republic of Ireland, Liechtenstein, Luxembourg, Norway, Portugal, Spain

Another and possibly fairer form of comparison is to discover how many museums each country has per million of its population. This produces quite a different ranking order.

11

Finland	124	Greece	41
Switzerland	106	Luxembourg	40
Austria	90	Germany, F.R.	39
Norway	85	Great Britain	39
Denmark	64	France	35
Belgium	57	Italy	33
Netherlands	55	Liechtenstein	23
Sweden	44	Portugal	20
Republic of Ireland	41	Spain	20

These figures are not, at first sight, easy to explain, although it is interesting to notice that the first six of the countries in this list have what appears to be the winning combination of a small population and a high per capita income. Small, prosperous countries tend, in other words, to have the highest ratio of museums to population.

It is worth mentioning, perhaps, that the prosperity of some of these countries is a relatively recent phenomenon. Until 1945, Finland, Sweden, Norway and Switzerland in particular were not notably affluent countries. Their economic rise is a post-war affair and it can be no accident that the growth in the number of their museums has coincided with this.

But the presence of a relatively large number of museums in a thinly populated country gives rise to certain problems. Museums have to be supported and maintained after they have been established, which means, in a country like Finland, that if they are to be successful, local people must cherish, visit and use their museums to an exceptional degree – the museum must take on something of the function of an all-purpose community centre – and municipalities and the State must give to their museums a financial priority which would be considered remarkable in a larger and possibly less truly democratic country, such as a France or Britain.

The post-war growth of museums in Britain requires some special explanation. Two out of every three museums in Britain today did not exist forty years ago and already doubts are being expressed and questions asked. Is this huge number of museums really desirable or necessary? Is it possible, even with the help of modern marketing skills, to find sufficient customers for more than 2,000 museums, when six or seven hundred were considered sufficient before the great museum boom got under way in the 1950s? Will the evidence of gradual impoverishment become steadily more noticeable with each year that passes? Will the money be there, whatever its source, to make it possible for even a majority of our existing museums to maintain themselves properly and to keep abreast of current and ever-changing tastes and demands? In a period of increasingly savage competition in the leisure market, will those museums which show their age too obviously lose public support to such an extent that they will find themselves compelled to close?

These questions are being asked all over Europe, not only in Britain. The next ten years will show whether the increase-curve is going to flatten, or perhaps even to fall. Perhaps museum deaths will begin to equal or conceivably to exceed museum births. There are certainly those who would regard this as a sign of increasing cultural health, rather than of a decline in vitality. Could it be that we have been guilty during the last few decades of a misguided and obsessive interest in our national past and that an excessive proportion of every European country's national resources has been devoted to preserving and exhibiting historical relics? Should we perhaps be devoting more time and energy to the present and the future and less to the past? Is it possible that what we need today is not more museums, but more effective museums, more relevant to the needs of our time?

Anyone who makes it his or her business to study Europe's museums objectively and as a whole will soon become aware that the typical museum is not the Musée d'Orsay in Paris, the Rijksmuseum in Amsterdam or the Deutsches Museum in Munich. These giants, employing hundreds of people and with annual budgets of millions of pounds, are exceptional institutions. In every country the type of museum most frequently found has a staff of no more than twenty and often considerably less. The problems and the opportunities facing such a museum are quite different from those with which the giants have to deal. Many, perhaps most, of them are seriously understaffed and underfin-anced. In 1988 the present author visited five new museums in different parts of Sweden. The permanent, paid staff at each consisted of a curator, always a woman, a secretary-handiwoman and a caretaker-technician. All the other work was carried out by volunteers. When the curator is on holiday or, as must sometimes happen, ill, there is no competent person to take her place. The museum has to get on as best it can. This is a familiar situation throughout Europe today and those who say that it is a conse-quence of too many museums chasing too little money have a good deal of evidence to support their case.

But there is undoubtedly another and more encouraging side to the picture. During the past forty years the American habit of supporting one's local museum by means of unpaid work – the volunteer system – in addition to gifts of money, has crossed the Atlantic to an impressive degree and made possible what could otherwise not have taken place at all. The concept of a museum as a community venture exists quite widely in Europe today and only the most conservative could argue that this is a bad thing. In country after country today one finds volunteers cleaning and repairing objects which may range from clocks to boats, undertaking secretarial work and guiding duties and acting as gallery attendants. Most museums who employ them in this way have paid staff as well, but increasingly frequently one comes across museums which are wholly run by volunteers. In Germany particularly it is not uncommon to find a museum where the building is provided and maintained by the municipality, which also looks after the heating, lighting and telephone costs, and where all the professional services are in the hands of volunteers. At least half and probably nearer to two-thirds of all the museums in the Federal Republic have no paid curator, a proportion which people outside Germany will find either shocking or remarkable, depending on the degree and nature of their involvement with the museum profession in their own country.

Volunteers, in the sense in which the term is used here, are not the same as Friends of the Museum, whose function is usually, but not always, limited to raising money. Most museums nowadays seem to have a Friends organisation, but normally only the smaller ones make use of volunteers. The thought of the Musée du Louvre or the British Museum relying on volunteer workers in order to carry out day-to-day tasks would send shudders through the official museum world in both countries, as well as provoking a serious trade union reaction.

One of the more remarkable features of the museum scene in Britain in recent years has been the spectacular growth of what it is customary to refer to as 'independent museums'. These are museums which have not been created by a local authority or by the State and they rely, more or less successfully, for their income on visitors' entrance fees, on profits from the museum shop and cafeteria, together with whatever they are able to raise in the way of grants from industry, private individuals and the public. More than a third of the museums in Britain are in this category, and in both France and Germany the figure is not dissimilar, although it is concealed by the fact that in neither of these countries is there any organisation, similar to AIM, the Association of Independent Museums in Britain, to look after the particular interests of such museums. On the Continent they are lone wolves. In the Scandinavian countries, with the notable exception of Finland, the privately organised and financed museum is still a cultural and political oddity and is viewed with considerable suspicion.

In Britain, the museum world undoubtedly owes a great deal to the independent museums. A high proportion of the new ideas which have revolutionised the way in which museums are run and thought about have come from this source and it is not difficult to understand why this should be so. An independent museum is wholly dependent on its ability to attract and please the public. Its director is in the same position as a theatre or concert impresario. If such a museum fails to attract visitors in sufficient numbers, it must inevitably die. State and local authority museums are not under the same constant, relentless pressure to succeed. For an independent museum, good marketing, good public relations, good management and, inescapably, a good product, are necessities, not luxuries.

The independent museums have been compelled by force of circumstances to concern themselves more with people than with objects. They have had to realise that they are in the communications business, and during the past thirty years their philosophy and methods have begun to filter into the State and local authority museums. The process has been slow and unevenly spread but, in general, the experiments and rethinking stimulated by commercial need have influenced British museums in a positive and fundamental way. And not only British museums have been affected by what one might perhaps call this new realism. A great many visits have been paid by Continental museum professionals to Ironbridge, Beamish, Styal, the Weald and Downland Museum and other leading independent museums in this country and ideas have crossed the Channel and the North Sea as a result.

Even so, however, museums throughout Europe continue to operate in a remarkably self-contained, national, if not nationalistic way. A museum in France has something specifically French about it and exactly the same could be said about the museums in every other European country, irrespective of their size or speciality. In museums, as in any other form of activity, ideas may cross political frontiers, but considerable adaptation is usually necessary before they strike root and grow. It would be a pity if it were otherwise and there is no reason to suppose that 1992, the year in which the European Community demolishes a large number of its national barriers, will change this particular situation very much.

Perhaps the most interesting and most far-reaching influence of the independent museums has been to weaken and possibly shatter the belief that a museum job is a safe job. In whatever country, employment in an independent museum depends very much on the needs of the moment. The budget cannot afford passengers and staff either have to adapt to changing circumstances or find another job. In local authority and State museums throughout Europe, including Britain, this is still not the case. Most professional staff expect and receive permanent employment, a system which is often not in the best interests of the museum, where the ability to get rid of idle and unsuitable people would be a valuable management tool.

But, in fact, the word 'management' has been accepted rather slowly and reluctantly in the museum field, although there are strong signs that the situation is beginning to change. With money increasingly difficult to obtain, a museum can no longer afford the luxury of a director or curator who regards managerial competence as inappropriate to a cultural institution.

A regrettable aspect of the present situation is the severe and apparently chronic shortage of funds to make it easier for museum staff to travel, in order to experience at first hand how problems are faced and solved in other countries. Directors, perhaps understandably, usually have first pick of whatever money is available, a policy which prevents people in the middle of their careers from receiving an intellectual stimulus at a time when they need it most, often in preparation for their last and most important post, as a museum director. There is strong evidence to suggest that money for this kind of travel is more difficult to come by in Britain than in most other European countries, producing a cultural isolation which is to the advantage of neither the individual nor of the country. Foreign travel, for those whose efficiency demands a constant renewal of their stock of ideas, is not a luxury.

In the case of Britain, this isolation is intensified by the deplorably low linguistic skills of most educated people. There is no reason to suppose that members of museum staffs are better or worse than the average in this respect. An attempt to discover which foreign languages, if any, were spoken either well or at all at six large provincial museums produced discouraging results. Those few people who claimed to speak a foreign language, usually French or German, proved, when asked to converse in it, to perform less than adequately. The British Museum makes the bold assertion that it has, on its large staff, people who, between them, can speak 'sixty languages', but even if one takes this remarkable statement at its face value, one is bound to wonder how many of these experts would be available, should their services be urgently required to deal with a linguistic crisis at the information desk. The same problem, presumably, would arise at the Musée du Louvre, which no doubt has a similar number of polyglot experts behind the scenes.

It is significant and sad to notice that at the Second Salon International des Musées et Expositions (SIME), held at the Grand Palais in Paris in January 1990, precisely two British museums or groups of museums were represented. Merseyside Museums had a stand and so, all honour to them both, did the National Galleries of Scotland. London, Cardiff, Glasgow and all the other major museum conurbations on this side of the Channel were all-too-conspicuously absent. The fact was duly noted, one hopes with shame and regret, by those official observers from Britain who went to Paris to inform themselves and especially the representatives of the Area Museum Councils.

In considering what we have called 'the situation in 1990', we have deliberately left the most important question, the quality of museum staff, until last. It is a truism which is not always true to say that one gets what one pays for, and the sad fact is that in most European countries people who work in museums are not well paid, a disadvantage which they share with teachers, librarians, and many other kinds of cultural workers. This has two serious consequences, the first that exceptionally well qualified, imaginative and energetic men and women tend to avoid museum work, and the second that many of the bright, ambitious people whom museums do manage to recruit soon leave for more rewarding work elsewhere.

There are, of course, exceptions. A great expert may find a post in a major museum a fruitful and agreeable base for his writing and consultancy work. A person of a retiring disposition may see behind-the-scenes work in a museum as providing the kind of skilled employment which his temperament demands, while to those who value security above all other considerations working in a museum offers the same kind of attraction as a job in the Post Office or the Civil Service. The nature of museum work has been undergoing a considerable change in recent years, however, and for better or for worse there are no longer the same opportunities to escape from the pressures of the outside world.

Broadly speaking, there are now, in every European country, two distinct types of professional museum personnel. Those belonging to Type A are found mainly in large museums. They are concerned almost entirely with research and with publishing the results of that research and, both in aims and in attitudes, they are not dissimilar to people pursuing similar objectives in universities. They are, if one needs a term to describe them, the museum academics. They have little, if any, contact with the general public. Type B consists of the bulk of those who work in museums at the professional level. They are the interpreters of a museum's collections, the people who plan and arrange exhibitions, run its educational services, look after the ordinary run of publications and in general act as the interface between the museum and the public. They are not necessarily unscholarly but, by force of circumstances, they have little time for that kind of research which has no immediate bearing on a particular exhibition.

Many of those who see themselves as belonging to Type A regard themselves as essentially superior to their Type B colleagues. More than a few of the Type B people are envious of those in the Type A category and would like to join their ranks. The distinction between the two is not, of course, absolutely clear-cut. In large museums, some Type A people do take a keen interest in exhibitions and are often used by Type B as advisers. But, in general, the two groups follow parallel careers and there is not a great deal of movement between one and the other.

The difference is compounded and in a sense confused by the various national methods of recruiting museum staff. In most countries – Britain is an exception – the tradition is to make appointments on the basis of academic achievement, even in the case of small museums. It has hitherto been reckoned that a successful applicant will learn the necessary museum skills in the course of carrying out his duties. This somewhat naive belief is now being increasingly questioned and rather more attention is now being paid to an applicant's personal qualities. Experience has conclusively shown that high academic attainments alone are no guarantee of success in a profession in which practical, business and public relations skills become more and more important each year. Expressions like 'training' and 'sharing experience' are heard a great deal more frequently nowadays than twenty or thirty years ago, but old traditions die hard. For some kinds of people, there is a lot to lose.

The pages which follow represent an attempt to forecast in what ways 1992, the next stage in the creation of the European Community, is likely to influence the situation described above, especially in Britain. Are we to expect rapid or fundamental changes or will developments continue to be gradual, piecemeal and to a large extent accidental? Will the mountain turn out to produce only a very small mouse or is the magic date likely to be much more than a symbol?

The study aims to provide reliable information not only about the theoretical effects of existing and forthcoming legislation, but about the way in which legislation is likely to be interpreted by each country, at both the national and the local levels.

The following questions are considered to be especially important.

1. What are the implications of the new legislation likely to be for British museums as a whole and for particular categories of museum?

2. How are the working conditions and prospects for individuals working in the museum field likely to be affected?

3. Are there any ways such as improving their language skills, in which people working in British museums could usefully prepare themselves for post-1992 opportunities?

4. Within the wider European context, what are the particular strengths of museums in Britain? Do these strengths need to be more widely and more effectively publicised abroad, in order to improve the employment possibilities for certain types of specialist?

5. What are the probable commercial opportunities and threats?

6. Is it possible or probable that 1992 will produce new sources of funding for museums in Britain?

7. Will it be necessary to develop new and improved forms of communication between museums and museum organisations in Britain and on the Continent?

8. Is it likely that there will be an increase in the number and variety of joint projects between European museums?

Section A
The Post–1992 Europe in which Museums and other Cultural Institutions will have to be operated

The Chairman of one of the major French banks said recently, 'Europe 1992 will make a difference because people think it will make a difference'. He might have added, 'because they hope it will make a difference'. 1992 is widely mentioned as if it had some intrinsically magic quality, a power to transform institutions and human attitudes. One may perhaps be pardoned for entertaining doubts about this. In most respects and in all the countries of the Community, life after 1992 will not be markedly different from life before it. 1992 is most unlikely to prove to be the millenium.

The most important question is probably whether France will continue to call the tune to the extent to which she has done so far. Anyone who spends time among Community officials in Brussels or in UNESCO circles in Paris is well aware that the culture of both these powerful institutions is French. Their way of going about their daily business, of reporting on their deliberations, of staffing departments, of organising and taking part in meetings, is French. If the headquarters of these bodies had been in, say, London or The Hague, their habits, hierarchies, priorities and forms of address would have been different.

    The Community as it has developed and as it is at the moment is an extension of French government and French bureaucracy. Its culture, the atmosphere within its buildings, derives from French traditions. Its non-use of Christian names within working hours is French. The structure of the Commission in Brussels was shaped by Emile Noël, its first and probably greatest Secretary-General and he created, with no noticeable opposition at the time, an environment in which any well-trained French Bureaucrat feels immediately at home and in which any Englishman, no matter what his calibre or his standing in his own country, can only survive and prosper by to some extent going native, by taking on protective French colouring. This is not merely a matter of speaking good French, although, as a means of self-defence, that certainly helps. It is a question of being willing to adopt a French sense of priorities, of seeing the world as a Frenchman sees it, and it will take a great deal more than 1992 to achieve this.

A succession of French governments and French representatives in Brussels has used the Community in an extremely skilful way. Far from being a threat to French nationalism, the Community has actually strengthened and enhanced it. Where Louis XIV and Napoleon ultimately failed, the less imperially-minded Jean Monnet may possibly have succeeded, by making it possible for France to dominate Europe. But, equally possibly, he may not. The crucial year for Europe may well turn out to be 1989, not 1992.

The upheavals in Poland, the German Democratic Republic, Czecho-Slovakia, Hungary, Romania and, more recently, the Soviet Union have changed the political, economic and cultural balance of Europe. It is impossible to think about the European Community in the same way as a result. Germany may have been on the fringe of the pre-1989 Europe. It is central to what is in the process of replacing it, as France is certainly not. By 1995, if not earlier, Berlin, not Brussels, may well be Europe's pivot and English is quite likely to have established itself even more firmly as the Latin of the new political system. There are two years to live through before one reaches 1992 and that year, announced so frequently and for so long as the year of Europe's destiny, may, when it comes, have a feeling of anticlimax about it. It may go down in history as a postscript to much more important and far-reaching events, rather than as something momentous in itself.

In any case, 1992, like the Community itself, is not in the first instance about culture or cultures at all. It is about making and investing money, about manufacturing, about trade. It came into being in the first instance because a small group of far-sighted people observed, in the chaotic and exhausted post-war world, that Western Europe, divided up as it was into national units that were California-sized at their biggest and rather less than Vermont-sized at their smallest, would be no match economically, militarily or politically for the superpowers of the United States, the Soviet Union and, as it shook itself free from wartime defeat, Japan. Its financial, industrial and commercial institutions would be unable to compete. Some form of grouping, amalgamation or integration was essential.

For France, Germany, Italy, Belgium and the Netherlands, the story of the European Community began in 1957, with the signing of the Treaty of Rome. For Britain, the cynic, the doubter, the country always on the fringe of Europe, giving daily thanks to the Almighty that it was protected by the Channel and Pharisee-like not as other Europeans, the key date is 1973, the year in which the reluctant bride across the Channel agreed to her marriage with

Europe. The British in general have never been completely happy about this, never really convinced that they did the right thing. For sixteen years, we have been arguing incessantly about the real nature of the relationship between Britain and the Continent, never able to agree as to whether our destiny lies in an integrated Europe or not, yearning nostalgically for the days of Empire Free Trade and wondering whether closer links with the United States might perhaps have suited us better.

Unless Edward Heath is thought to deserve the rôle, Britain has had no equivalent of the two Frenchmen and one Belgian who over the years have provided the Community with its vision and its driving power. There has been no British Jean Monnet, Robert Schuman or Jacques Delors, determined to bring the post-war dream of a united Europe to fruition. Schuman told the world 32 years ago that 'Europe will not be created at a stroke or according to a single plan. It will be built through concrete achievement.' Many people in Britain, including some in positions of considerable influence, have expressed their doubts about the concrete achievements so far. Somewhat unfairly, the British have been written off by other members of the Community as, at best, a nation of unbelievers and, at worst, a people who go to the European church only when it suits them.

Since they became members of the Community in 1973, the British may have suffered unduly, not by having doubts and suspicions, but by giving public expressions to them. The French have been more subtle, more skilled at hedging their bets. They have never really accepted the free trade, free markets aspect of the Community, but they have shown a remarkable talent for giving rhetorical support to such matters. They have always assumed that, if there should happen to be an agreed Community measure they disliked, they would find it possible to disregard or bypass it without too much difficulty. But in recent months the speed with which the Commission is now actually moving towards the Single Market it always said it wanted has caught many French officials off balance. They are aware – and it is an unfamiliar and far from pleasant sensation for many of them – that it is becoming harder for them to discover ways of avoiding the Commission's decisions. They retain their protectionist, anti-free market instincts, but they are beginning to realise that they may ultimately be forced to compromise more than they would wish.

One major reason for this change of position is that the Germans are becoming more confident with each month that passes. In 1957 they were economically and politically weak, still loaded with guilt stemming from the events of the Nazi period and the war, and consequently inclined to content themselves with a secondary policy-making rôle. Since then, however, they have become prosperous, their economy is well-balanced and apparently secure, and some form of German re-unification is clearly inevitable. What has hitherto been France's European Community may be in the process of transforming itself into Germany's Community and in this situation the support of Britain for one party or the other is a stake worth playing for.

It is not inconceivable that both France and Germany may to a certain, possibly a considerable extent, lose interest in the Community, and devote greater efforts towards cultivating economic and political links with the Central and Eastern European countries. This would not so much weaken the Single European Policy as divert energy and attention from it. To a French, German, or for that matter British firm with goods to sell, Poland or Czecho-Slovakia, for instance, might yield more profitable results for less effort than, say, Italy or the Netherlands.

The links between political power and cultural power are subtle and always interesting. In France they have been very strong for more than a century and never more so than at the present time. The French, especially in high places, have never made a secret of the fact that they consider their language to be superior in clarity and elegance to all others and since the end of the Second World War they have continued to fight a vigorous, but increasingly futile and unsuccessful, rearguard action against the spread of English as the major language of world communication and, perhaps even more serious, of diplomacy, where the supremacy of French was at one time unquestioned.

The French will, of course, continue to draw attention to the infinitely greater respect which they claim intellectuals enjoy in France, compared with England, to the enormous scale of France's subsidies to the arts and to that untranslatable activity known as 'urbanisme'. Where, they are likely to ask, is the equivalent in Britain or, indeed, anywhere in Europe, of the Musée d'Orsay, of the Pyramide and what lies underneath it at the Louvre, of the Centre Pompidou, of La Villette? Where is the urban concept to compare with La Défense?

Britain's, and possibly Europe's response to these Gallic cock-crows is very likely to be that Paris today is what it has always been, the great French showground, that Paris grows fat while the provinces starve. The Anglo-French mutual teasing goes on, generation after generation, and there is no reason to regret it because it enriches the cultural pattern of Europe. The disappearance or the weakening of cultural variety is the last thing one would wish to see happen. It is natural and normal to be proud of one's national culture and to want to share it, so far as this is possible, with foreigners. There is no reason to feel that the agencies which exist to publicise the French, British, Italian or American way of life are in themselves anything but beneficial, although the purposes for which they are used are occasionally not as worthy as they might be. In general, the British Councils, the Goethe Institutes, the Instituts Français and the rest do a useful and much appreciated job in the foreign countries where they operate. They help people to learn the language and to understand something of the country where it is spoken, they provide much-needed libraries and they arrange educational visits. Their aim, briefly expressed, is the normal task facing a diplomat, to make his country better understood and better liked abroad. If this has political consequences or, as it has been well expressed, if trade follows the literature and the music, one can hardly feel that a crime has been committed. It seems perfectly reasonable that, nationally as in one's private affairs, one should buy from people one likes, rather than from those one dislikes. The British Council operated successfully in Europe long before a Common Market was thought of and there will continue to be a need and a welcome for it after 1992.

This is another way of saying that 1992 is not going to mark the end of European nationalism or of attempts to promote national cultures abroad. Each Goethe Institut and each Institut Français is, in effect, a department of the German or French embassy in that particular country, and nobody has yet thought fit to suggest that one of the consequences of 1992 is likely to be the suppression of embassies and ambassadors.

But embassies are an old story and one takes them for granted. It is the international agencies and organisations which steal most of the limelight nowadays, and community, in all its contexts and shades of meaning, is a fashionable word. The European Community takes its place by the side of the Moslem community, the Jewish community, the gardening community, community care, the prison community, and all the other warm-sounding expressions which draw strength from the appealing concept of togetherness.

It is misleading to consider the European Community on its own, as if it were the only or the most brightly coloured pebble on the European cultural beach. Three distinct organisations are helping to build the framework within which museums will be operating during the next decade. They are ICOM, the International

Council of Museums, the Council of Europe and the European Community. This seems a suitable moment to take a general and critical look at the achievements of all three of them.

ICOM came into being in 1946, shortly after the establishment of the United Nations Scientific and Cultural Organisation (UNESCO). Philosophically and financially, it was closely associated from the beginning with UNESCO. It described itself as 'a professional organisation devoted to museum development throughout the world', and said that 'it represented the museum profession internationally and is a technical partner in the execution of UNESCO programmes in the field of museum development'. It has never, perhaps wisely, made any serious attempt to define 'the museum profession'.

ICOM held its first General Assembly in Mexico City in 1948 and has continued the practice every three years since then, moving around the world as it does so. It has a network of national committees, of varying degrees of activity and efficiency, publishes a newsletter and maintains, at its headquarters in Paris, a documentation centre, based on the large number of museum books, periodicals, catalogues and reports which are received each year. The documentation centre is in two sections. The first consists of the material in its original form, as received, and the second brief details of these items, stored on the computer.

ICOM's headquarters is seriously underfinanced and understaffed and the space available for its activities is inadequate. For these various reasons, there is a considerable time-gap between receiving accessions and processing them. Those using the documentation centre in the Rue Miollis will find a friendly welcome, once the tight security at the building has been penetrated, but must be prepared for slightly chaotic conditions on occasion.

The Triennial Programme adopted by the General Assembly of ICOM at The Hague in September 1989 sets out professional and trusteeship objectives over the next three years . It reaffirms that museums have duties towards the collections they hold in trust, to the natural and cultural inheritance and to the people of the communities they serve. It believes that in many countries better training and more fruitful and regular contact between museums and government are required if the cultural inheritance is to be adequately protected. It wants to see tougher government legislation regarding the import, export and transfer of the ownership of cultural property and, equally, it believes that more needs to be done within the profession to make sure that museums are managed in an ethical way, so that their collections are adequately safeguarded.

ICOM has also made clear that what it calls the national inheritance cannot be properly protected from theft and illegal sale in the absence of reliable inventories of museum collections and of objects outside museums. One cannot protect what does not officially exist.

The Council of Europe was born two years after ICOM. In 1948 the Congress of Europe, representing 26 countries, met at The Hague. It called for the creation of a united Europe, including a European Assembly. This was the origin of the Council of Europe. The Statute of the Council was signed in 1949 and came into force two months later. The founder members were Belgium, Denmark, France, Ireland, Italy, Luxembourg, the Netherlands, Norway, Sweden and the United Kingdom. Between then and 1978, eleven other countries have joined – Turkey (1949), Greece (1949), Iceland (1950), The Federal Republic of Germany (1951), Austria (1956), Cyprus (1961), Switzerland (1963), Malta (1965), Portugal (1970), Spain (1977) and Liechtenstein (1978). The Secretariat is based in Strasbourg.

Membership is available to those European states which 'accept the principles of the rule of law and of the enjoyment by all persons within their jurisdiction of human rights and fundamental freedom'. This limitation has until very recently excluded the Eastern bloc countries, but it is likely that the application of Poland and Hungary to become members will be received during 1990 and of Czecho-Slovakia and the German Democratic Republic in 1991. By 1992 it is quite possible that the Council will include the whole of Eastern and Central Europe, except the Soviet Union and Albania, a situation which few people would have expected in 1949.

The Council has an inter-governmental Committee of Foreign Ministers, which has powers of decision and of recommendation to national governments, and a Consultative Assembly – the Parliamentary Assembly – which consists of 170 members, who are either elected or appointed by their national parliaments. In addition to these two bodies, there is a large number of committees of experts. Two of these, the Council for Cultural Co-operation and the Committee on Legal Co-operation, have a certain amount of autonomy.

The Assembly has no legislative powers, but it has a fair claim to be considered the conscience of Europe, by voicing its opinions on important current issues. These are reflected in resolutions. The Ministers' function is to translate the Assembly's resolutions into action within their own countries. About 130 Conventions and Agreements have so far been concluded. These have included cultural affairs, the conservation of European wildlife and natural habitats and the protection of the archaeological heritage.

The Council's funds come entirely from its member governments and are approved on an annual basis. It organises a number of international conferences each year, some of them within the cultural field, it supports institutions and initiatives, such as the European Cultural Centre at Delphi, and it makes awards – the Council of Europe Prize within the European Museum of the Year Award scheme – is a good example – but it does not normally make grants for individual museum projects.

Its operations within the museum field are looked after by the Committee on Culture and Education in Strasbourg, which has a small, but highly efficient staff of permanent officials, who generally see working for the Council as their career.

The European Community or, as it was during its early years, the European Communities, was the last of the three organisations discussed here to come on to the scene. In 1950 Belgium, France, the Federal Republic of Germany, Italy, Luxembourg and the Netherlands began negotiations which it was hoped would give Europe, through the merging of national interests, a greater chance of peace in the future. The process began in 1951, when the signing of the Treaty of Paris created the European Coal and Steel Community (ECSC). The European Economic Community (EEC) and the European Atomic Energy Community (Euratom) followed in 1957, when the two Treaties of Rome were signed. The United Kingdom, Denmark and Ireland became full members in 1973, Greece in 1981, Spain and Portugal in 1986, and Luxembourg in 1987.

Until 1967 the three Communities were completely separate, each having its own executive, the Commission, and a decision-making body, the Council. In 1967 they were merged, to form the European Commission and the Council. The Commission has 17 members, serving for four years. It acts independently of particular countries, in the interests of the Community as a whole. The Council of Ministers is made up of the Foreign Ministers of the 13 national governments and represents the various national interests. It is the body which takes decisions under the provisions of the Treaties. The European Parliament consists of 518 members, directly elected by the member states. It has a right to be consulted on a wide range of legislation. It can reject the Community's annual budget as a whole and it can amend items of non-obligatory expenditure.

The European Investment Bank was set up in 1958 under the Treaty of Rome in order to contribute to the balanced development of the Common Market. It can grant loans, help the development of less advanced regions, finance modernisation and development and encourage the improvement of communications between member states.

The original three treaties were amended by the Single European Act, which came into force in 1987. The Act provides, among other things, for majority voting, instead of unanimity on a number of issues and for a wider and more effective rôle for the European Parliament. If the majority of nations are in favour, it is now possible for the Community to move outside the economic sphere and to involve itself in social and cultural matters.

Of the 17 Commissioners and the Directorates for which they are responsible, five are of particular relevance to the problems and opportunities of museums. They are:

(a) DGX Films, television, culture, Community public relations

(b) DGXI Environment

(c) DGXIII Telecommunications and information

(d) DGXVI Regional policy

(e) DGV Training and education

The Directorates could hardly be described as a band of brothers. They do not talk to one another a great deal and they are engaged in fierce battles over money and power. Directorate (a) – DGX – has also shown signs of jealousy towards the cultural activities of the Council of Europe and of a wish to take over some of its power and influence.

The British Government has not been particularly helpful to the Community so far as cultural matters are concerned. It is its unchanging and apparently unchangeable view that the objectives of the European Community are strictly economic and that consequently the Community has no power to act in the cultural sphere. Many people, however, want the European Community to be concerned with more than money and employment and at the end of 1987 the Commission presented the Council and the Parliament with a document called, in the English version, *A fresh boost for culture in the European Community*. It is an action-plan for the period 1988-92.

This is concerned with five main fields and envisages co-operation with the Council of Europe. The fields are:

A. The creation of a European cultural area

This would give a high priority to the free movement of 'cultural goods and services' and to the 'development of cultural provision'. It would involve an agreed and more satisfactory definition of 'national treasures' and an inter-Community code of ethics in the art trade. The United Kingdom, under alleged pressure from some of its major auction houses and dealers, has the reputation of being unreasonably hostile to this.

B. Active encouragement of the European audio-visual industry

C. Access to cultural resources

This includes improving linguistic ability, preservation of the cultural heritage, including museums and galleries, sites and monuments, and outstanding buildings.

D. Training

The Commission wishes in particular to improve training for cultural administration, on which there are very few courses at university level.

E. Dialogue with the rest of the world

The document was discussed informally by the Ministers of Culture in 1987–88. They decided to give priority to audio-visual matters, to the promotion of books, to sponsorship and to training. No formal proposals however, have so far been made to the Council by the Commission.

What it has done is to set up a Committee of nine Cultural Consultants, each of whom chairs a sub-committee on a particular subject. There is, for example, a sub-committee on museums. A fairly general comment made by people serving on the Committee and the sub-committees is that fundamental issues have rarely been tackled and that the policy seems to be to concentrate on action which will bring the maximum publicity and the minimum political risk.

On the higher levels of administration, working for the Community is not usually seen as a career. Secondments and temporary appointments are normal. People come and go and continuity is not easy to achieve.

1992 is not about the elimination of national differences, cultural or otherwise. It is concerned, or should be, with the abolition of barriers to the free movement of goods, people and money. It has to do with the harmonisation of standards, taxes and legislation, with the right of people born and brought up in one country to seek work in another, with the ending of irritating and time-wasting Customs delays. Whether this should all lead towards a political integration of the countries making up the Community is a matter of lively debate at the present time.

The Single European Act, signed by all the member states of the Community after the Luxembourg summit in 1985, is a declaration of intentions. The implementation of these intentions is partly a matter of interpretation, partly a matter of practicality and partly a matter of circumstances, which may change very considerably between now and 31st December 1992, which is when the Act is due to come into operation.

The Act specified eight basic aims:

1. By 1992 there shall be an entity known as the internal market. This is defined as 'an area without internal frontiers in which the free movement of goods, persons, services and capital is ensured in accordance with the provisions of the Treaty'. Member states shall, however, retain 'the right to take such measures as they consider necessary for the purpose of controlling immigration from third countries, and to combat terrorism, crime, the traffic in drugs and illicit trading in works of art and antiques'.

2. Steps shall be taken to reduce the administrative and legal constraints on small and medium-sized businesses.

3. European monetary union is to be an EC goal, 'progressively realised'.

4. Disparities between richer and poorer regions of the Community are to be reduced by means of the Community's funds.

5. The European Parliament is to be allowed to amend legislation through a second reading and in certain cases, mostly commercial agreements, to have the final word.

6. Technological research is to be encouraged along agreed lines.

7. The Community is to take action to improve the environment and help to protect human health.

8. The leaders of the Community countries undertake to formulate and implement a European foreign policy through consultation.

Of these aims, 1, 2, 4 and 7 certainly and 6 possibly could obviously have important consequences for museums, especially if they could be persuaded to regard themselves as cultural business, which in today's world they inescapably are. Within this broad framework, a large number of general provisions have been made. In effect, they remove from each country the right to make relevant decisions themselves and enforce the recognition of agreed Community standards. The most important are:

1. Agreed minimum health and safety standards, in food products and drugs.

2. 'Essential technical standards' for all sectors of the economy, including the construction, automobile, civil engineering and chemical industries, and for financial services.

3. The complete abolition of all internal frontier controls.

4. Public bodies will be required to open all supply contracts worth more than £134,000 and all public works contracts worth more than £3.3 million to cross-border competition.

The second and fourth of these provisions clearly have implications for museums. By insisting on high specifications, the cost of building work might well increase and it is conceivable that both State and municipal museums could find their paper clips, floor polish, electric light bulbs and showcases coming from strange sources after 1992.

After this, most of what the Community plans is mostly of only indirect interest to museums in Britain or anywhere else, although the members of the staff of, say, the City Museum, Norwich or the National Portrait Gallery may decide to move their personal account and possibly their mortgages to a branch of the Crédit Mutuel or the Dresdner Bank in a year or two's time.

Having got rid of internal barriers to trade, the Community then proceeded to safeguard its external frontiers.

5. National import quotas will be replaced by Community-wide quotas.

6. The Commission intends to make reciprocal agreements with its main trading partners, particularly in the field of financial services.

7. It is expected that American and Japanese companies will set up branches in Europe, to protect themselves against the effects of 1992.

8. Anti-dumping duties will be imposed on foreign companies who are unfairly undercutting the Community market.

Broadcasting and film production are to be protected against competition from outside the Community.

9. Broadcasters will be compelled to devote a specified proportion of their air time to feature films made in Community countries.

10. Satellite broadcasters will be permitted to transmit programmes anywhere within the Community, provided they meet certain requirements.

There will be considerable changes in the financial, banking and insurance systems.

11. All restrictions on the movement of capital, within the Community, are to be abolished.

12. Any High Street bank may operate throughout the Community on the basis of a single licence.

13. Cashpoint bank cards will be standardised.

The Commission also hopes to see an expansion in the use of the European Currency Unit and the establishment of a European Central Bank.

Certain company activities are to be supervised and controlled.

14. There will be a comprehensive merger control, giving Brussels the power to approve or refuse all large-scale mergers which have 'a European dimension'.

15. The Commission will continue to try to discover and assess Government subsidies to companies, in order to prevent anti-competitive practices.

16. There will be a Community trade mark, a European patent law and harmonisation of national audit and fiscal procedures.

Close attention is to be paid to transport, the principal measures being:

17. Air transport within the Community to be more competitive.

18. Greater freedom of entry for independent operators on the main European air routes.

19. Abolition of the system of national quotas for the road haulage industry.

20. European road haulage companies to have complete freedom of destination within the Community.

21. Duty-free allowances for travellers to come to an end.

There are, in addition, a number of regulations regarding the professions which will be dealt with in the next section. Their intended effect is to enable people classified as professionals, with mutually recognised qualifications, to practise anywhere in the Community.

If the Commission's aims and plans are realised, and it would be wrong to under-estimate the opposition to them in some quarters, people and money should be moving much more easily and normally around most of Western Europe at the end of the 1990s than at the beginning. The loosening-up process is already well advanced in some forms of activity. It is most noticeable, perhaps, in the construction industry, which could be considered a microcosm of future developments over a wide field.

Public works contracts are not particularly profitable on the Continent, where the margins are generally less than one per cent. In Britain they average nearer two per cent and the difference is attractive to firms based on the other side of the Channel. The new EC rules for large public sector contracts throw such projects open to competition within the Community, with severe penalties for failure to allow a fair contest. With this in mind, and in the knowledge that very large contracts are certain to come up during the next decade for expanding the London Underground, building new motorways and widening others, and putting Britain's drainage and water-supply systems to rights, Continental firms have begun to spend their way into the British market, either by taking a minority interest in companies or by buying British concerns outright. Major British contractors, on the other hand, have been abandoning low-profit civil engineering in Britain and transferring their expertise in management contracting for office and housing projects to the Continent, taking a fixed percentage for their services. Management contracting linked to building on time and within a budget has become a British speciality and the rewards are excellent .

This two-way export trade is likely, too, to have interesting results so far as staff are concerned. A German contractor, for instance, is most unlikely to bring building workers from Germany in order to construct a new Underground line in London. He will employ British labour for the job and, in order to get the best, he is quite likely to pay something closer to German rates. British technicians, on the other hand, may discover openings for themselves in the firm's design and planning offices at their headquarters in Mannheim or Hamburg or wherever it may be.

This situation can be paralleled in many other fields. The member states of the Community, in other words, are poised to take in one another's washing, once the Single European Act becomes law in 1992. But, underpinning the Act are certain developments which have nothing directly to do with Community decisions at all. One of the most important of them is the Channel Tunnel and the new railway system which will allow it to function and to make money. The European determination to modernise and extend its railways is likely to be as important as any of the Commission's plans. Even more significant is the willingness of individual countries to provide funding for it, an attitude which contrasts strangely with that of the British government.

No-one yet knows, of course, exactly or even approximately what cross-Channel business the Tunnel is likely to attract, in the matter of both freight and passengers. No-one will know until it actually opens, but it seems unlikely that it will not lead to a very different pattern of transport between Britain and the Continent. One aspect of this which has been curiously neglected so far is its possible effect on what one might call leisure pursuits.

Let us consider two possibilities, a day and an evening out in Paris and a similar trip to Brussels. We are told, and it may well be true, that the new lines at present under construction on the Continent, but not yet, alas, in England, will make it possible to get from the centre of London to the centre of Paris in three hours, a time which is considerably better than one can achieve at present by air, even under very favourable circumstances. Given such speed and given reasonable fares, there is no reason why a substantial number of the citizens of Paris, Brussels and London should not spend from 11 in the morning until 9 in the evening in one another's capitals, visiting, shopping and generally amusing themselves, without the strain of driving and parking or the exorbitant cost of an aeroplane seat, which in fairness the Community says it is determined to reduce. Even more important, perhaps, would be the knowledge that their journeys would begin and end at the times they were supposed to, without the miserable and frustrating delays caused by fog and the tantrums of air traffic controllers. These trips would be weatherproof. The mechanics would be predictable.

And there are other possibilities. By 1992 the new Euro-Disneyland, south of Paris, should be open and ready for business. It has been estimated that, in order to justify the huge international investment that will have been made in the venture, it must attract at least ten million visitors a year, and during 1989 full-page advertisements have appeared in newspapers throughout the Community countries to show how this will be achieved. Diagrams are provided to show that, once the Channel Tunnel is open, 17 million people will be two hours away from Disneyland by car, 41 million within a four-hour range and 109 million should be able to drive there in under six hours. By air 310 million could manage the journey in two hours or less. On the basis of the American Disneyland experience, the organisers reckon that one in forty of the people within the Euro-Disneyland catchment area could be expected to make the pilgrimage to this 20th-century Mecca each year. Each visitor is expected to spend about £150 at present prices, for a two-day trip and the promotors' skill will lie in providing good value for that sort of money.

Most people will probably go as family groups and they will be prepared to sacrifice and to save for the sake of the experience. However, money which goes in one direction cannot go in another and Disneyland's gain is certain to be somebody else's loss. The main losers may be Alton Towers and similar theme-parks throughout Europe and the main winners, apart from Disneyland itself, are likely to be the airlines, the hotels, Eurotunnel and the coach companies. Shuttle services to Charles de Gaulle from several points in Europe, with a bus connection from there to Disneyland, are a real possibility.

The main importance of Disneyland, however, is that it will accustom huge numbers of people in many countries to think and up to a point plan their lives on a European scale. How far this will increase the prestige of France, the host country, is difficult to forecast. There is always a possibility that this great new tourist attraction will appear to those who visit it to exist in a no-man's land and that its French surroundings will appear irrelevant, just as Spain and Spanish culture seem irrelevant to those who take their holidays on the Costa Brava. But that it is destined to become one of Europe's major focal points and possibly its greatest Tower of Babel seems certain. It may just be, of course, that the venture will not succeed. Europeans, after all, are not Americans and they may not be prepared to travel considerable distances in huge numbers in order to have a day out. Short of a severe economic recession, however, that possibility seems somewhat remote.

Disneyland is not the only enterprise in the entertainment and leisure industries to be thinking on a European scale. The American film makers, MCA Universal Studios and British Urban developments, a consortium of 11 construction companies, are jointly planning what they call 'a movie-inspired spectacular', to be built either on 1600 acres of Rainham Marshes in Essex or on a site of similar size at Melun-Senart, south-east of Paris. What is called 'the park and attraction' would be based on a similar project which is now being completed by MCA near Orlando, Florida, and which is causing nearby Disneyworld some concern.

Visitors will be able to stroll around streets which will form the backdrop for films and television productions, as well as watch programmes being made by MCA Universal. The park will have 14 rides, based on film classics like Jaws, ET and King Kong, all of which will be designed by Stephen Spielberg. They will certainly be out of the ordinary. The King Kong ride, for instance, will have the giant ape catching and shaking the passenger-filled cable car before dropping it 100 feet.

The project is expected to attract five million visitors in its first year. The catchment area will certainly be as wide as Disneyland's and it is always possible that some families will decide to see Disneyland and Universal City on the same visit. Like Disneyland, Universal City has no fear of failure.

By the time one reaches 1992, certain trends which are noticeable at the moment may have become something more than trends. Large-scale migrations from one Western European country to another are extremely unlikely, but the habit of having a main residence in country A and a secondary one in country B may grow to a point at which it causes a significant number of people to modify their culture. Working from Monday morning to Friday in country C and living from Friday evening to Sunday evening in country D may be increasingly popular. International chain stores and chain hotels may begin to change the face of towns. Holidaymakers may at last begin to desert the beach and the sea and to explore the interior of countries in serious numbers. The tourist industry may learn how to cater for people who prefer to travel north, away from the sun and the heat rather than towards them.

Predicting how human beings will behave in even five or ten years' time is a risky business and to assume that Europeans will react in the way the Community expects and wants them to react is a little unwise. What businessmen may want is not necessarily what the ordinary citizen wants and what is good for lorry drivers may be very bad indeed for Customs officials. Some, possibly many, of the provisions of the Single European Act may well be bitterly resisted and possibly sabotaged as people begin to see how they work out in practice. Nations, like individuals, cherish their differences and their prejudices and one cannot get rid of attitudes with which one has been surrounded since infancy merely by passing an Act. One can decide in Brussels that doctors and lawyers are free to work where they like, but every Frenchman knows that doctors who are not French are nothing more than quacks and every German is convinced that only German lawyers are real, properly-trained lawyers. Many English people suffered an initial sense of outrage when they heard that, because of a serious shortage of the home-bred product, London children were to have young, fully-trained, English-speaking Germans to teach them when they returned to school in the autumn of 1989. In its way, the case of the German teachers in British schools is a parable of the Community. With rare exceptions, only when a need is real and proved beyond all doubt will foreigners be allowed to fill it, no matter what the Community may say and whatever dire penalties it may threaten for non-compliance.

Post-1992 Europe is a Europe of imponderables. All that is certain at the moment is that European 'harmonisation' in 1992 will provide the industrial and commercial communities with easier access to customers in other parts of the EC. But, although Europeans will increasingly adopt similar political values and similar social aspirations, they are extremely unlikely to begin to lead similar lives, to adopt other cultures. 70 per cent of adults in the Community countries speak no language but their own. To reduce this to 60 per cent within 20 years would be a remarkable achievement.

The only cultural heritage that the 321 million people of Europe share is that of America. That is why the organisers of Euro-Disneyland and Universal City are on very safe ground.

A spokesman for Universal City has recently spoken of 'the shared film heritage' and that, alas, is probably more of a reality than the shared European heritage.

Section B
The Professional consequences of 1992 for Museums in Britain

A museum professional, broadly speaking, is a person who performs other than mechanical, manual or purely routine tasks in a museum. The museum profession is composed of such people. Neither definition is foolproof, but more satisfying alternatives are difficult to find. They are at all events adequate for the present discussion.

One must, however, be careful to include in the category of professionals those highly skilled people who carry out work comparable to that of a surgeon within the fields of medicine. To classify a surgeon as a manual worker simply because he works with his hands and in this way to equate him with the hospital cleaners would be absurd. He has to have an immense body of knowledge at his command before he can be trusted to use his hands and it is the combination of hand and brain, of experience and physical capacity, of theory and practice, which makes him a professional. A museum conservator is in exactly the same position. To be entrusted with the restoration of a Rembrandt or a Greek vase carries the same degree of responsibility, in museum terms, as having a damaged human body in one's care. A conservator is clearly, by any reasonable definition, a professional.

Which other types of museum worker are also entitled to be thought of as professionals is a matter for discussion. One needs to be flexible in such matters, but it is as dangerous and unhelpful to think of everyone who works in a museum as a member of 'the museum profession' as to think of a printer of sheet music as a member of 'the musical profession' or a ward cleaner as a member of 'the medical profession'. One has to discriminate in order to avoid devaluing the currency.

What has to be admitted straight away is that there are no statistics which show either the number of museum professionals or the total number of employees in the museums of the member states of the Community. Reasonable calculations suggest, however, that the Community's 13,500 museums may provide a living between them for about 300,000 people, of whom about half, at a generous estimate, could be classed as professionals. It is not a large number and its modest size may come as a considerable surprise to many members of the profession itself. 150,000 men and women do not,

38

it might be thought, possess a great deal of political influence or bargaining power. As voters, their respective governments could afford to disregard them – they are much less numerous than journalists or schoolteachers, for example – were it not for an important factor which has to be brought into the argument. Museum professionals are responsible for the care and display of what survives from each country's past. They are caretakers of history and, as such, they cannot be disregarded. Their function is out of proportion to their numbers.

But the museum profession, allowing that such a thing exists, is in no country a society of equals. Status and power is divided in two ways. The director of a large national museum, say the British Museum or the National Museum in Copenhagen, has a higher prestige and therefore more power than the person in charge of a small museum in the provinces. And the head of an art museum is more highly thought of than the head of any other kind of museum, mainly because, in the public mind, an art museum is associated with 'treasures', with objects which fetch enormous sums at auction sales. The market value of the collections rubs off on the person who looks after them and adds to them.

For these reasons, the museum profession anywhere in Europe is really more than one profession. There is very little similarity between the daily work of the Keeper of Egyptian Antiquities at the British Museum and the Curator of South Molton Museum, although both would consider themselves to be museum professionals and both, in their different ways, are doing a useful job. One could say very much the same about teachers. A master at Eton and an assistant at an East London comprehensive are both teachers, and both spend their working hours among the young, but the differences between the two jobs are probably greater than the similarities.

If one visits a large number of European museums each year and talks to the people who work in them, one soon becomes aware of basic grievances, call them Eurogrumbles, and of hopes and plans for the future. The question, "What are the professional consequences of 1992 likely to be for museums in Britain?' – one could usefully add 'or elsewhere' – therefore needs to be reworded. One should perhaps be asking 'What is 1992 going to do, if anything, to make the lives of Europe's museum professionals more rewarding, more fruitful and more satisfying?' Before one can attempt an answer to this question, it is necessary to set out a list of the principal dissatisfactions and aspirations, as they have been presented year after year and in country after country to this particular observer of the museum scene. In doing this, one has to remember that people come into museum work, as into any other kind of employment, for a variety of reasons, some because they see it as a useful base from which to do academic work, some because they prefer objects to people, some because they are fascinated by the process of communication, some because they enjoy bringing order out of chaos, some because they find an enormous pleasure in handling old objects and in feeling the past come alive in their hands, and some, alas, because they need a job and can think of nothing else or better to do. 'I was,' said the very successful director of an important museum in Mexico, 'a Jesuit priest in Belgium. One day I woke up and found I had lost my faith, so naturally I turned to museum work.' The point and moral of the story lies, of course, in the word 'naturally'.

Both the hopes and fears of museum people are most effectively recorded in the way they were expressed, in the first person, as quotations.

'I have been here long enough. I've learnt all I can here and done all I can do. I know it's time I made a move, but I've been making applications for more than a year now and nothing happens.' (*Scotland*)

'I was trained as an art historian and when I became Director here 20 years ago I was very happy, especially after we got this splendid new building. But I find myself more and more being forced to do things that simply aren't me, fundraising, looking at useless computer printouts, attending so-called 'management' meetings. I've decided to retire early and I can't wait for the day.' (*France*)

'I've always been interested in machinery, but like most museum people here, I was trained as an art historian, You have to, if you want a museum job here. It's like studying Latin if you wanted to be a priest in the Middle Ages.' (*France*)

'We've got a huge new building and one of the biggest and finest archaeological collections in the world. But the professional staff consists of just one person, myself. I've got no assistant, and if I'm ill or one of my children is, I have to stay at home and leave the museum to anyone who happens to be around.' (*Italy*)

'I reckon I've done a good job in creating this museum from scratch and the public seems to like it. But we're terribly under-staffed and under-financed and when I talk to the Assistant Mayor about it, he doesn't seem to understand what I'm talking about. He doesn't like women, anyway. All he cares about is rugby and

Freemasonry. He's not a cultured person at all,. That's why he's responsible for education and culture, to keep down spending on these things.' *(France)*

'You'd better talk to the Mayor yourself when you have dinner with him tonight. He's a nice enough man, but all he cares about is *having* the Museum. The town's got its museum, that's all that matters to him. It's what goes into the tourist brochure. I can't convince him that I need more money to staff it properly and run it.' *(Sweden)*

'No, we haven't got a shop or a café. You're not allowed to, if you're a museum in the public sector. The local shops wouldn't like it and you might make a profit, which would give you a certain amount of independence.' *(Italy)*

'I'll tell you why we get such poor people coming up as museum directors nowadays. The pool hasn't got good people in it. They all left years ago, in their twenties. They couldn't live on the money and they couldn't see why they should have to face a lifetime of penury.' *(England)*

'When it's a matter of building work or equipment or of money to buy pictures, I can get anything I want. But there isn't a penny for the extra staff I desperately need. They don't think people are important.' *(Belgium)*

'50 per cent of my professional staff are absolutely useless. They're not interested in museums, they're not interested in the public, they're not interested in anything. But they're Civil Servants and immovable. I inherited them. I can't get rid of them and I've got to pay them until they retire. I could do wonderful things with the money.' *(Austria)*

'In my country, an independent museum is considered almost obscene. I ought to know. I run one.' *(Sweden)*

'I haven't seen as much of museums in other countries as I should have, but they won't let me have time off even to go to a conference. If I go, I have to take it as part of my holiday. But the Director's always going abroad. Why does he need it more than I do?' *(Austria)*

It would be unfair, of course, to say that these quotations and the situations they reflect are an adequate reflection of the museum situation in Western Europe today. But they are a guide to grievances, none of which are likely to be removed by any changes which 1992 may bring, except perhaps in a very indirect way. If the

41

Commission's policy and regulations should happen to result in a considerable increase in prosperity, either in the Common Market as a whole or in particular countries, then some part of that increase might be available to improve the situation of museums and that in turn might produce more contentment among those who work in museums.

As matters stand at the moment, there is no general shortage of people qualified and willing to work in museums. Supply and demand are roughly in balance, which is another way of saying that, of rare specialists, the bargaining power of museum professionals is low. If, however, more money were to be made available to museums and if the standard of qualifications were to be raised, a shortage could easily occur. A further factor to bear in mind is that, in relation to the national cost of living, museum staff are not well paid anywhere in Europe. Only in exceptional circumstances is a museum person likely to improve his or her standard of living merely by going to work in another country. According to where one comes from, working conditions may in some respects be better in certain other countries and holidays may be slightly more generous. Chief among the exceptional circumstances are obvious promotion and the odd specialist niche which does not exist in one's own country. A number of people, even so, may wish to take a post abroad for a time in order to broaden their experience or for the sake of the stimulus of spending time in a very different working atmosphere. In the course of visiting Continental museums during the past ten years, this observer recalls meeting British members of their staffs only five times, once in Italy, once in Holland, one in France (Paris), once in Germany (Berlin) and once in Luxembourg. All five people were unmarried and all were about 30. None had experienced any problems in obtaining work permits. None intended to spend more than a few years in the job. All were on short-term renewable contracts. Three were women and two were men. All spoke the language of the country well.

One has a suspicion that these five may constitute a composite portrait of people who work in museums abroad in the future, single, in early to mid-career, mobile and with above average linguistic ability. One would hope and expect that, suitably encouraged, the number of such adventurous transients will greatly increase, but it would be quite unrealistic to expect large numbers of museum professionals of any nationality to uproot themselves and their families semi-permanently in order to seek a new life in some other part of the Community. This would demand at the very least a 'harmonised' European pension scheme and social payments, of which there is at the moment absolutely no sign, and a safety-net guarantee, in the form of a job back in one's own country, in case the experiment failed.

Secondments and exchanges, for perhaps one or two years, are quite another matter and it is in these fields that common sense indicates the most likely future of museum internationalism to be.

It has been recognised for many years that the Community's single European market could not work properly unless there were a single market for labour. There had to be freedom to move around at will in search of better conditions of employment and new types of opportunity. Article 57 of the Treaty of Rome, as amended by the Single European Act, obliged the Council of Ministers to issue directives for the mutual recognition of 'diplomas, certificates and other evidence of formal qualification', so that anyone who qualifies in one member country is allowed to work freely in another. The implementation of these directives is likely to prove far from easy, however, mainly because of different national traditions of education and the fact that professions and skills are essentially nationally based. Considerable progress has, however, been made and it is anticipated that a European Vocational Training Card will be introduced during 1990, certifying that the person holding it possesses a vocational training qualification universally recognised throughout the Community.

So far as the professions are concerned, the Directive relating to the Vocational Training Card and to the freedom to use it in order to practise is subject to four guidelines.

(a) The Directive applies to all professions for which a three-year university degree is required.

(b) Mutual recognition is based on confidence and trust between member states.

(c) Recognition is given to 'the finished product', which is defined as a fully qualified professional, who has successfully completed any additional training required after obtaining a university degree.

(d) Where there are important differences in training between one member state and another, the appropriate national authorities are empowered to check the competence of an individual by means of an aptitude test or a period of probation. The Commission dislikes this condition, suspecting that some professions in some countries may use it as a means of maintaining a closed shop, and is watching the situation carefully.

Thirty-eight professions in Britain are affected by the Mutual Recognition Diploma. They include librarianship, but not museum work, for the very good reason that there is as yet no way of comparing the qualifications, if any, that museum professionals are required to hold as a condition of employment. Consequently, in 1990 a librarian in Britain will be able to show a prospective employer on the Continent his Vocational Training Card, but a museum professional will not. He would be a bold person who believed that this situation was likely to change in any material respect during the 1990s. Whether this means that museum people are going to be second-class citizens of the Community as a result only time will show.

One needs in such matters to maintain a sense of realism and proportion. It is most unlikely that in any of the thirty-eight professions there will be a flood of men and women wanting to use their Vocational Training Card. Most people are perfectly content to work in the country in which they were born and brought up and in which they trained. Emigration is an exceptional act, mostly confined to those who are either desperate or greedy. The Commission already has some evidence of the general wish of professionals to stay where they are. For some years, as a result of an earlier Directive of the Council of Ministers, doctors have been free to work anywhere in the Community, but so far, out of a total of 600,000 doctors practising within the Community, only 2,000 or one in 300 are not working in the country in which they qualified. There is no reason to suppose that the proportion will eventually be greatly different for any of the other professions.

So far as museum work is concerned, the early resolution of the training problem would seem to be of considerable importance. Without a mutual recognition of museum qualifications between member states of the Community, people who work at the professional level in museums will be at a considerable disadvantage. All that can be done here is to indicate what is happening within the Community countries at the present time in the matter of training and what the prospects are for the immediate future. The most thoroughgoing, although not necessarily the most satisfactory system is to be found in France, based on the Ecole du Louvre.

The Ecole du Louvre is subtitled, 'école du patrimoine culturel', which could be roughly translated as 'school of the cultural heritage'. Museums are indeed concerned with the cultural heritage, but an examination of the course offered by the Ecole du

Louvre makes it clear that 'cultural heritage' is defined in a somewhat narrow and old-fashioned way. The emphasis of its teaching is heavily on archaeology, ethnology and the fine and decorative arts.

Within this framework, there is offered a three-stage course. The first stage lasts for three years and is open to students possessing the baccalauréat or its equivalent. All students are required to follow a course in the history of art, which continues throughout the three years. In the second year they also have lectures on the history of technology and in the third on the history of collections. On the successful completion of this course, they receive a 'first stage diploma' ('diplôme de premier cycle').

The second stage is open to students who have done sufficiently well in the first stage and is devoted to museology, that is, to 'the principles and practice of museography, the management and administration of museums, the scientific study of works of art and their conservation and restoration'. There is an examination and a thesis, and, if the results of these are satisfactory, the reward is a diploma in higher studies ('diplôme d'études supérieures') or, for students who have been admitted on the basis of qualifications deemed to be equal to the first stage diploma, a special diploma in museology ('diplôme spécial de muséologie').

The third stage, like the first, lasts for three years and is concerned entirely with research. After the successful submission of a thesis, a student is granted the Research Diploma of the Ecole du Louvre.

The Ecole du Louvre has a second function, to spread knowledge of the 'patrimoine culturel' among members of the general public and to this end it organises an extensive programme of lectures in Paris and in the provinces.

The system in force in France results in a two-tier organisation of people working in museums at what would, in Britain, be considered a professional level. Anyone who has passed satisfactorily through the first two stages of the Ecole du Louvre course is eventually entitled to be appointed 'Conservateur de musée'. He is 'at the centre of the cultural life of his city' and has total charge of a museum operating in the public sector. He, and only he, is considered to be a museum professional. All other museum directors or curators, and there are many of them, have received no professional museum training. They are 'amateurs', no matter how much experience they may have had. They have learnt on the job. They lack the all-important dimension of theory.

These further points should be made about the French course. The first is that most of the students who are registered for the second stage are by then working in a museum. For a proportion of those who are not, scholarships are available. The second point is that both stages 1 and 2 involve a considerable amount of practical work on assignment in museums, under the close supervision of a reasonable local conservateur de musée, who will refer to his students as his 'stagiaires'. This practice of tutoring involves experienced people from all over France in the system and prevents it from being over-dependent on Paris. Point three is that a respectable proportion of the students, usually about 5 per cent, come from outside metropolitan France, usually from one or other of the former French colonial territories. There is also the occasional student from other countries, including, very exceptionally, England. Since the work of the Ecole du Louvre is carried out entirely in French, students without a sufficient knowledge of this language necessarily cannot be admitted. And point four is that there is a good deal of dissatisfaction in France about what is increasingly felt to be the undue emphasis given to art history in the course and to the failure, nationally, to provide training of equal quality and status to prospective students whose background is in science, engineering or natural history. There is a strong possibility that a new school of museology for this kind of person will soon be founded elsewhere in France, possibly in Alsace.

It is at present difficult to see exactly who in France would be officially submitted as being worthy of receiving a Vocational Training Card from the Community. Would it be only someone who was qualified to be a Conservateur de Musée or would other categories of person be considered?

In France, as in all other countries, courses are provided at various types of Further Education Colleges for boys and girls who wish to embark on a career as what would in Britain be called conservators, that is, people who possess the skills and the knowledge required to restore and conserve objects. Those who qualify as a result of such training are, however, generally thought of, and paid, as technicians, not professionals. The fact that some of them, working as independent craftsmen and not as museum employees, earn considerably more than salaried museum professionals, does not, as yet, appear to affect the social prestige of conservators.

There is a certain irony in the situation in that, as technicians, museum conservators may receive their vocational training card, at least in some countries, earlier than 'the professionals'.

One should remember, perhaps, that the majority of people in French museums today who are working at the professional level do not possess the Louvre diploma. This includes more than a few conservateurs de musée, who were appointed before the present strict regulations applied. Are all these people to be thought of by the Commission as unqualified? No-one has yet ventured on an answer to this awkward question.

Of the other countries within the Community, Britain approaches closest to France in the matter of museum training, although there are profound and obvious differences between the two. Of these, the most important is that the French emphasis on the history of art does not exist in Britain, not because British museums are staffed by art-haters, but because the museum tradition on this side of the Channel has always been more broadly based. Those who intend to make their career in art museums are very likely to follow a course at the Courtauld Institute, where the atmosphere and the product bear a strong resemblance to what one finds at the Ecole du Louvre.

Until now, the premier courses available in Britain for museum professions have been those organised by the Department of Museum Studies at the University of Leicester. Since the Department was established in 1966 it has, in the Department's own modest words, 'become the backbone of professional training in Britain and a model for new university departments in other parts of the world. Over 500 postgraduate students and, since, 1980 nearly 300 in-service Diploma students have undertaken post-graduate museum studies and professional training at Leicester University.' These students have included a number from abroad, which in recent years has been considerably higher than the Ecole du Louvre's 5 per cent. These have mostly come from English-speaking countries, but there have been others. Denmark, Spain, Ireland and even France have all sent students. The courses are, of course, conducted entirely in English.

The Department of Museum Studies at Leicester offers a range of courses and qualifications. There is now a Foundation Course, which has been launched with financial help from the European Community's Social Fund. For this, candidates from Community countries who are unemployed and under the age of 25 are eligible for grant aid to enable them to become students. In addition, the Department has its Diploma in Museum Studies and a course leading to a Master's degree.

Among British universities, Leicester is not unique in providing postgraduate museum studies. The Department of Art History at Manchester University, for example, has been offering a postgrad-uate Diploma in art gallery and museum studies since 1971 and the

Institute of Archaeology, which is linked to University College, London, has had a Master's degree in Museum Studies since 1986.

On the Continent, a number of university departments, mostly of art and archaeology, offer, or purport to offer, a museum component within their first degree courses, but this appears to consist mostly of visits to museums and galleries and of a discussion of the display techniques which are used there. Gothenburg, in its Archaeology Department, does rather better.

What is now being offered at Leicester in its two-week modular courses is not markedly different from what one finds at the Louvre. It could not, one might say, be very different. Museums have certain needs and certain habits wherever they may be, and the business of a museology course is to prepare students to meet these needs and habits. The style of the syllabus may vary from country to country but the ground covered will be much the same.

Leicester offers Museums in the Modern World and Museum Management. So does Paris. Leicester offers Collection Management. So does Paris. Leicester offers Material Culture: Objects and Collections. So does Paris. Leicester offers Communication and Interpretation. So does Paris. Leicester offers Specialist and Curatorial Options. So does Paris. Leicester offers Museum Attachments and Experience supplemented by Course Work. So does Paris.

Leicester, not unlike Paris, is catering for the top end of the market and until now far too many people working in museums, at all levels, have not been satisfactorily provided for in the matter of training. It is this situation which the new independent Museum Training Institute has been set up to correct, so that what are called 'all sectors of the museum community' are able to find a form of training suitable for their needs. If things work out well, the new Certificate in Museum Practice should leave few museum employees outside its net.

What Britain will then have are two methods of producing qualified museum staff, the Certificate in Museum Practice, which is not university-based, and a Diploma in Museum Studies, which is. Anyone possessing either the Certificate or the Diploma would presumably be entitled to the European Community's Vocational Training Card.

The only other institution in Western Europe which approximates to Paris, Leicester, Manchester and the Institute of Archaeology in London is the University of Umeå, in Northern Sweden.

At Umeå, where the Director in charge had previously created and run a highly successful innovative museum of regional and cultural history, there is a one-year postgraduate course, arranged on a modular basis. Students are required to study the history of museums, in Sweden and abroad, the theory and principles of museology, the techniques of conservation, exhibition design, museum management, and the planning and operation of a museum education programme. There is both a written and an oral examination and a diploma is awarded to successful students.

Some of the students so far recruited for the course already have museum experience, others do not, but the assumption is that all will eventually make a career in some form of museum work. Teaching is conducted in Swedish, but most of the books on the reading list are in English and foreign specialists, speaking usually English, French or German, regularly give lectures to students and take part in seminars. The probability is that, as the course develops, most of the students will be Swedish, but there could be some from other Scandinavian countries and just possibly from elsewhere too. Sweden is not, of course, in the European Community and whether a Umeå diploma would be ultimately recognised for a European Vocational Training Card is difficult to say.

The Reinwardt Academy in Leiden has been running courses for people working in museums since 1976. Since 1987 its museum department has functioned as the Museological Faculty of the Amsterdamse Hogeschool voor de Kunsten. It now organises a four-year course, the entrants to which are required to possess similar qualifications to those which would gain them admittance to a university.

Students follow courses in the history of art, museology, museum communication, exhibition techniques, conservation, cataloguing and documentation, cultural history, archaeological methods and techniques, and museum education programmes. During the first and second years they also have to spend an appreciable amount of time studying English and Dutch. There are excursions to museums within Holland in the second year and to London and Paris in the third. A diploma is granted at the end of the course.

Foreign students are accepted, provided they have an adequate knowledge of Dutch, but so far there have been very few of them, except from the former Dutch East Indies.

Most other countries in Western Europe have some form of training available for museum professionals, but it is usually neither systematic nor obligatory. In Spain, those working in museums at the more responsible levels are brought together in

Madrid by the Ministry of Culture for a more or less linked series of three-day courses on themes such as 'Recent developments in museums'. Teaching on those courses is by means of lectures and discussions and there is usually an opportunity to hear an expert from outside Spain. Between 50 and 100 people usually attend each course.

Portugal has a similar system, although much less money is available for it, and in-service training exists in Denmark, the Republic of Ireland (at University College, Dublin), Norway and Sweden, where the University of Gothenburg runs courses and meetings. The situation in Germany is complicated, because each Land is responsible for its own cultural and educational programmes. There is no Federal Ministry for such matters, and in practice what happens is that such training as exists is looked after by the Land Museums Association, an organisation of museum professionals. There are university post-graduate courses, as for example at Mainz, but they tend to be of a theoretical nature and not to be greatly valued by people in the profession.

One might sum up the situation in Western Europe by saying that it is still normal, except in France and Britain, to choose professional museum staff on the basis of their academic attainment and to reckon that they will pick up the necessary vocational skills in the course of time and by watching, listening and experimenting. To what extent both the museums involved and their visitors are any worse for this is a matter of opinion and faith. It is unwise to assume that all training is necessarily a good thing. Under certain circumstances it can result in a stereotyped, if not standardised product, frightened of behaving in an unconventional way. He would be a bold man who claimed that Germany's museums, run by people largely without a formal training, were worse than those of France, where training is centralised and tightly controlled, and where power goes only to those who have been brought up in an approved manner.

'The usual practice in Germany for people who work in museums,' says one internationally famous director, who himself came up the hard way, 'is that they go directly from the university, where they studied, for example, art history or history, to the museum. They learn nothing of practical work in a museum during their time at the university. They are, as we say, dropped into the cold water and they have to learn to swim in it. They may work as a volunteer in a museum for a year or two, but you can also start directly as a curator or director, if you are lucky enough to get the job.'

One needs to remember that training, in museums as in other fields, is an industry in itself and it is in the interest of people who work in that industry to exaggerate its importance. It is also in the interests of the museum profession itself, as in the legal profession or the medical profession, to move towards a closed shop, to which only those with approved qualifications are admitted. But, as one knows from other professions, the closed shop is no guarantee of quality. The fact that one passed an examination twenty years ago says nothing about one's present effectiveness. There should, theoretically, be no idle, out-of-date, irresponsible doctors or lawyers, but experience shows that there are all too many of them. To maintain standards in any profession, what is required above all else is the power to terminate employment. Security of tenure can be the greatest enemy of quality and efficiency and there is no reason why museums should be an exception to the general rule.

It should go without saying, however, that termination of employment should be a step of last resort in the attempt to raise standards and maintain enthusiasm. In-service training throughout one's career is at least as important as the basic training which formed the prelude to that career. It could be that 'training' is not the best word for this process, since what is really involved is the opportunity to become acquainted with new technologies, new financial structures, new methods of marketing and administration, and above all, with new attitudes to the job. Anyone who takes part in what has come to be known as in-service or on-going training soon realises that much the most important feature of such sessions is the opportunity which they give to participants to measure their own experience and knowledge against that of other people. Much of the provision of the Museum Training Institute is likely to be in this field and, provided the necessary funds can be discovered, the inclusion of non-British experts in seminar and lecture programmes will provide a very desirable injection of new ideas into what can otherwise so easily become an incestuous and self-righteous activity.

Perhaps the most important aspect of in-service training in any profession is the extent to which it is made obligatory. A combination of stick and carrot is what is required. The stick can be of the simple, bludgeon variety, as in Spain, where professional museum staff, at all levels, are told which courses they are to attend and when, their expenses, of course, being paid. But there are other possibilities, such as an increase in salary for those who have attended a cycle of seminars and passed an examination or submitted a satisfactory thesis at the end of it, or who have successfully completed a course in a foreign language. In extreme cases, when one is dealing with the totally idle and unwilling, the termination of employment may be the only answer, but the existence of such a weapon should be clearly understood. One should not, however, be afraid of using such a sanction. It already exists in other fields. In the Netherlands, for instance, specialised teachers of foreign languages who cannot produce evidence that they have spent a certain minimum period of time within a period of five years in the country whose language they teach lose their licence to teach. This undoubtedly helps to maintain the very high standard of language teaching for which the Netherlands is justifiably celebrated.

One might perhaps sum up the probable and possible effects of 1992 on the museum profession, whether in Britain or anywhere else, in this way.

1. No directive of the Commission is going to increase the number or character of jobs in museums. All that can happen is a change of attitude, a different sense of priorities, on the part of governments and the tax-paying public.

2. Since museums are, like any other activity, subject to the law of supply and demand and since there are, in every country, more people who want to work in museums than places available for them, one must expect a high degree of nationalist feeling in making appointments. Whatever the Commission's rules may be, foreigners are likely to find themselves welcome only in those fields where for one reason or another, there is a shortage of native candidates 'of suitable quality and experience'.

3. People with an exceptional skill will find no great difficulty in getting a job abroad, should their inclination go in that direction and should the financial and prestige incentives be great enough. They would need to be bribed to move. Given present national salaries and cost of living rates, there is no marked financial reason for British museum professionals to work in other European countries.

4. For practical reasons – family commitments, housing, schools, pension arrangements – one is most unlikely to find a substantial number of museum professionals in Britain or any other Community country wanting to move abroad, either temporarily or permanently, after 1992.

5. By comparison with other countries, museum professionals who do wish to move abroad are going to find themselves at a

disadvantage compared with the members of other professions. There is as yet no mutually agreed evidence of competence.

6. British museum professionals will continue to find their poor linguistic ability a serious barrier to working abroad. There is a strong case for including a language module in the courses leading to the Certificate in Museum Practice.

7. The greatest value of 1992 is likely to be a speeding up of the present trend towards more short-term visits abroad on the part of museum personnel and students. The Community's Erasmus scheme, which gives financial help to students wishing to study in more than one country, is a valuable contribution to a greater degree of internationalism in education and training. The Department of Museum Studies at Leicester should certainly benefit from this and there will no doubt be other instances.

There are those individuals, institutions and countries which believe that the best form of training lies in the ability to exchange ideas. The Spanish Ministry of Culture proceeds on this assumption, so far as its museum employees are concerned and it seems an approach to be welcomed. One cannot treat experienced people in the same way as raw recruits.

The main forums for the interchange of ideas would appear to be:

(a) Exchange visits by both groups and individuals. These can be either short or medium term.

(b) Lectures and seminars by foreign professionals at training courses, such as those held at Leicester, Umeå and Leiden.

(c) Subject conferences. These already take place on a European scale, organised by specialist organisations, such as those concerned with maritime museums, open-air museums and transport museums. The Council of Europe is also active in this way, with major conferences on such themes as Museums and the Natural Environment and Museums and Education.

Excellent as these occasions may be, they share a fundamental weakness, which is that the people who attend them are nearly always directors or curators of museums and, less often, heads of museum departments. People lower down the ladder are not well served in this respect.

Financial help given by the Community to (a), (b) and (c) above, especially in the matter of travelling expenses, would be likely to have a benefit out of all proportion to the costs.

Section C
The Commercial and Financial implications of 1992 within the Museum Field

During the past thirty years or so, Britain has been Europe's principal laboratory for the organisation and management of museums on sound commercial lines. The reason for this is simple enough. Britain has what is, by European standards, a remarkable number of so-called independent museums, operated for the most part as independent trusts. These must either balance their books or go out of business in a very short time. Since there are now getting on for a thousand such museums, their effect on the national pattern of thinking is great and since their number includes some of the most visited and most publicised museums in the country, and since some of the brightest people have been working in them, the influence of their philosophy and methods has inevitably been considerable, especially since the organisation which represents them, the Association of Independent Museums (AIM), is a well-run and publicity conscious body. It is AIM, rather than the Museums Association, which has set the pace in recent years, with its frequent and excellent conferences, its series of practical publications and, above all, by its general attitude to the planning and administration of museum work. No other European country has anything resembling AIM. Where independent museums exist on the Continent, they exist on their own. They do not constitute a movement, with its own particular philosophy, as they do in Britain.

Ideas which began in independent museums have gradually spread throughout the system, their origins often being forgotten in the process, and the best of these innovative places, untrammelled by obsolete traditions, have been visited by first a trickle and then a flood of museum pilgrims from abroad, anxious to catch a breath of the new and invigorating wind blowing through the museums of Britain. What they found is now in the process of being modified and adapted to make it suitable for acclimatisation elsewhere. It is impossible to over-estimate the tonic effect which Britain has had on Europe's museums during the post-war period.

An important part of this effect has been that museum directors are now increasingly thought of as managers, rather than, as previously, scholars. The new breed did not originate in Britain, one should perhaps point out. It was an American creation, but Britain gave it a European face and probably made its transplantation to the Continent a good deal easier than it would otherwise have been. Somewhat ironically, the museum-manager became indispensable only when it was realised that museums had insufficient money to allow them to compete in the leisure market, where the bulk of their visitors would henceforward be found. They had to raise their sights in order to attract and hold customers and, as a consequence, the traditional easy-going, non-commercially minded museum, the 'dusty old museum' which had such deep roots in the popular imagination, began slowly to disappear. It is still far from dead, but it no longer represents the norm. The museum with only six visitors a day is not acceptable any more. A museum's collections are now increasingly looked on as its assets and the owners expect an adequate return on the investment. With the members of the public, who are taxpayers as well as potential visitors, and with their immediate masters, the ministries and local authorities, the museums have to be seen to be offering value for money, and this demands a different kind of person, with a different set of attitudes, to run them.

With hindsight, one is beginning to understand what an important contribution Britain has made during the past two decades to the development of the concept of museum management. There is no doubt that new movement began in certain key museums outside the public sector – Ironbridge, the Weald and Downland Museum, the National Motor Museum, and the Gladstone Pottery Museum are good examples – where young and intellectually adventurous directors saw very clearly that their own and the museum's future was closely bound up with the need to use capital in an imaginative and profitable way. Previously, words like 'capital', 'investment' and 'assets' had never been used in the context of museums, except in America, where there had never been any shame in viewing a museum as a business enterprise, basically the same as a department store or an airline, but selling a different kind of commodity.

The influence of Ironbridge and the other business-minded pioneers spread rapidly throughout Britain's steadily growing number of independent museums during the 1970s and 1980s and then further afield, as their directors began to move into publicly-funded museums. The most celebrated of them, Neil Cossons, who had made his name as virtually the creator of Ironbridge, went to run, first, the National Maritime Museum and then the Science Museum. His transition both symbolised the fact that the previously almost Berlin-Wall type of career barrier between the publicly and privately financed museums had been breached at last, and brought a person with a well-developed business sense into an area where it had previously been conspicuously lacking and even scorned. There was, inevitably, powerful resistance to Cossons' entrepreneurial and cost-cutting approach but he felt encouraged by the knowledge that he would find support in high places. He has become an international figure, but in his essentially pragmatic turn of mind he has remained totally British. In his passion for efficiency, his hatred of waste, his salesman's instinct to go aggressively after customers and his determination to give value for money, he is not the traditional museum director at all. With one foot in the Establishment camp – he is, after all, a member of the Athenæum – and another in the penny-watching, make-do-and-mend world of the independent museums, he is an indispensable bridge-figure in the process of thinking about museums as businesses. His future may, of course, not lie in museums at all, and his successor may well come from a quite different field. Indeed, one of the most interesting features of the European museum world of the 1990s is likely to be the appointment to responsible posts in museums of non-museum people with good industrial and commercial experience. This has already happened in Britain and there is every reason to expect that the trend will continue and spread. Such people will not necessarily spend the rest of their career in museums. They may well move backwards and forwards more than once between the commercial and cultural sectors. A good manager is a good manager and he looks for his opportunities where he can find them.

1992 is essentially about industry, commerce and money, not about culture, which is regarded as a fringe activity. Museums will benefit only in so far as they are able to key themselves into the new economic climate and learn to benefit from it. This must involve talking the language of money, which many people working within the educational and cultural fields find distasteful, difficult and even degrading.

The essence of a successful businessman is his ability to cut costs in a creative manner, to make investment yield the highest possible return and to be constantly on the lookout for ways of increasing productivity. The new-style museum director will have much the same list of priorities, but they will be only a means to an end, to achieve a better museum, more highly regarded by the public than would otherwise be possible. The problem for him then becomes that of buying the goods and services he needs in the most favourable market he can find. The intention of the Commission with 1992, especially in its public procurement policy, is clearly that everyone with money to spend should be completely free to comb the countries of the Community until he finds the best bargain, but the problem is likely to lie in the definition of phrases such as 'most favourable' and 'the best bargain'.

This is well illustrated by what happens in the case of important architecture projects. In recent years, a number of prestigious museum contracts in Community countries have gone to foreign architects – art galleries in London (American), Stuttgart (British), Düsseldorf (Danish) and a museum of avant-garde furniture at Weil, on the German side of Basel (American). These instances are quite exceptional. There is great pressure on governments and local authorities to restrict their choice to French architects, if the building is in France, to Italian architects, if it is in Italy, and so on. The reasons for this are not financial. A big and important public building, it is felt, should be a symbol of the architectural profession of the country where the building is to be, and the rule has been only rarely broken. Foreign architectural firms have frequently been invited to compete for the job, but reasons are afterwards found for preferring the work of a native architect. One of the most impressive recent instances of this was the new National Library in Paris, where the final choice of architect was made in accordance with the known personal preference of the President, who felt that it would have been a disgrace almost amounting to treason if a foreign architect had been selected for such an important national monument.

It seems most unlikely that any Commission directive or the Single European Act will influence this situation greatly, if at all. For reasons of prestige, the very well-known architects will continue to win some foreign contracts. The rich countries like it to be known that they have a James Stirling building or two in their collection, just as the large art museums cannot lift up their heads without possessing a handful of Picassos or the odd Reynolds or Rembrandt. But for most of their work, every country will go as before to the architectural firms which are more or less on their doorstep. There is little reason why they should not and every reason why they should. An important building is not merely a matter of an architect with a name. A contract of any size requires a properly equipped office and a staff able to work in the language of the country. Some of the largest architectural and construction firms in Britain may consider it worthwhile to set up branch offices in this or that country abroad, but probably few will find the investment a sound one. In any case, museums alone would not pay the bills. France and Germany build perhaps three new museums every year and Italy possibly two. There is simply not enough new museum work around to keep an office busy on that alone.

With designers, the prospect is more encouraging, in that far more museums are being refurbished and redesigned each year than built from scratch. Here again, however, one has to issue a caution. On the Continent it is quite normal for the architect responsible for modifying a museum building or for producing a new one to get the contract for all the design work as well. The architect-designer is rare in Britain, but frequently found abroad. It is true that British designers, like British architects, might find it worth their while to attempt to compete on price, but the differential would have to be very substantial to make success probable.

There are only three design practices in Western Europe which work almost entirely on work for museums. These are the businesses headed by Robin Wade and Pat Read in London, Hans Woodtli in Zürich and James Gardner, also in London. All of them are wholly concerned with the interiors of museum buildings, with the design of exhibitions. They are designers, not architects. All have as much work as they can handle. The Robin Wade practice works entirely in Britain and Ireland at the moment, although in the past it had commissions in Australia. James Gardner, on the contrary, has done very little in Britain and prefers to concentrate on major projects abroad, usually outside Europe. Hans Woodtli has plenty to do in Switzerland, where money is abundant and museum growth has been very rapid during the post-war period. He is able to accept foreign contracts from time to time and has been working recently on a major project in Albania, where Swiss neutrality has been a considerable political advantage to him. The Woodtli business, Werberei Woodtli, is remarkable and possibly unique, in that it consists of two autonomous sections, one dealing with museum design and the other with industrial and commercial advertising. The two businesses share photographic and other technical services. With its multilingual staff, speaking and corresponding in French, German, Italian and English, Werberei Woodtli is equipped to take work in other countries in a way which the Robin Wade and James Gardner practices are not.

Contractors and sub-contractors could be better placed. If the price is favourable, there is no reason why a museum in, say, Marseille, Heidelberg or Utrecht should not employ someone in Peterborough or Exeter to carry out its building work or supply materials or components, always assuming that any linguistic problems had been overcome. It is worth mentioning, perhaps, that anything with a low value to weight or bulk ratio is unlikely to be able to compete with more locally-produced items where the transport distances are long. Bricks and cement would, in general, be out, display cases and audiovisual materials might be in.

One then comes to the materials, equipment and services which museums buy, either regularly or occasionally. These range from writing paper to vacuum cleaners and from floor polish to slide projectors and, if the terms are good, there is no reason why British suppliers should not get their fair share of the business available. All that 1992 can do to help in this is to ensure that the Community regulations concerning procurement are observed both in the spirit and the letter.

Most museums are short of money, some chronically so. Is the Community likely to be able to do much, if anything, to ease this burden? The short answer is no, but this answer is subject to certain qualifications. It is believed in some quarters that there is a lot of money available in Brussels for cultural purposes. This is most certainly not so. The Cultural Department in Brussels is very small, compared with other sections of the Community's bureaucracy and, relative to other activities, it operates on a very small budget. Its chief weakness, however, is that most of its staff is employed on short-term secondments from member states and that continuity of both policy and its implementation is not easy to ensure. Enthusiasms tend to come and go with individuals.

There is no shortage of instances of this. In the late 1970s, the then head of the Cultural Department, who was French, conceived the imaginative plan of setting up, with Community money, a chain of what were called European Rooms in museums throughout the Community's area. The idea was that each Room should illustrate the historical links between other parts of Europe and the region in which the museum was situated. The museums were to be in places where there was a good balance of visitors between tourists and local residents, an above average all-the-year-round attendance, and an active, enterprising museum management. For various reasons, some of them political, Norwich Castle Museum, in Eastern England, was chosen. An interesting exhibition was created by the Norfolk County Museum Service and, with some refurbishment and up-dating, it continues to attract visitors today.

Very soon after the exhibition opened, the head of the Cultural Department retired and his project retired with him. There were no other European Rooms and in 1989 no-one in Brussels had any memory or record of the experiment. The beginning was also the end.

The Community's intentions in cultural matters are undoubtedly good and individual projects within the museum field will continue to be supported. If present procedures are any guide to the future, these conditions should be kept in mind:

1. Schemes are unlikely to be approved unless it can be shown that they affect more than one member country. The Museum Rooms met this criterion.

2. A considerable, often strangely considerable amount of detail will be required to accompany the application, even when the amount of money is very modest, and candidates without the necessary determination and stamina may well decide not to proceed further.

3. Speed in dealing with the application is not to be expected. Brussels moves at a bureaucratic pace and with proper Civil Service decorum. Any museum in Britain which requires Community money for even the most worthwhile project should make itself aware of the rules of the international game and be prepared for a long wait.

There are those who are wondering whether the coming of 1992 will result in any increase in the amount of money available to museums through sponsorship channels. It probably will, although it would be wrong to encourage exaggerated hopes in this direction. The experience of recent years has shown that most firms, even the big multinationals, keep away from international projects and much prefer to sponsor projects in a single country. A German motor manufacturer of high repute will put money into a season's bullfighting in Barcelona and into a new art gallery in Stuttgart, because it believes, probably rightly, that this policy, of following national fashions, will win it friends and favour in each country. IBM, one of the world's most generous and imaginative sponsors, has hitherto shown itself to be more than a little wary of museums, preferring schemes where the emphasis is on the future rather than the past. It has, however, paid a large sum for the construction of working models of Leonardo's inventions and for their permanent exhibition in the castle at Vinci, near Florence, and it sponsored the European Museum of the Year Award for four years, a public-spirited act in which it was followed by another major international concern, the accountants and management consultants, Arthur Andersen.

For most industrial and commercial firms, however, charitable investment begins at home. Most of the Community's museums of any size could now point to some sponsorship activity from which they have benefited during the past five years. Art exhibitions are particularly in vogue among major sponsors. Henry Moore, Picasso and Hockney are felt to confer status and prestige on the company, steam engines and natural history less so, although concern for the environment is beginning to run a close second to the major artists. There are fashions in these matters as in all others and the wideawake museum director makes it his business to be aware of them.

Few of Europe's largest industrial and commercial concerns are without a foundation of some kind which takes part in sponsorship activities. Apart from IBM, which in every European country is the first name which seems to come to everyone's mind when the possibility of sponsorship is mentioned, BMW, Lufthansa, Volkswagen, Fiat, Heineken, ICI, Carlsberg and Moët et Chandon all maintain important foundations. ICI, with a European headquarters in Brussels, is anxious to raise its Continental profile and is consequently moving closer towards what might be called the IBM position, beginning to look favourably on sponsorship possibilities away from the centre of its empire in London. All the others, however, still show a strong inclination to support cultural ventures only in their own country, although where sporting activities are concerned, they are occasionally prepared to go further afield. An exception has to be made for major art exhibitions, which, for reasons of company prestige, are considered internationally to be at the top of the museum tree.

It is possible that the economic changes brought about by 1992 will change the pattern of sponsorship to some degree. If a French company buys up a British water company, it may well decide that it is in its interests to ingratiate itself with the local community in Britain and sponsorship is an obvious way of doing this. If German or British banks decide on a major expansion of their network of branches in other countries, they could possibly follow a public relations policy which included a measure of local sponsorship. A Japanese car manufacturer, with a new factory in Spain, built to make it possible to enjoy the commercial advantages of the Common Market, might deem it prudent to devote a small fraction of its profits to cultural pursuits in the district in which it had based itself.

All these developments are more or less certain to increase in the near future. They are merely a projection of what is happening already. But sponsorship is showing signs of adopting new and more enterprising forms and to be expressing itself in terms of people, rather than naked cash. In more than one country, large concerns are beginning to second members of their staff to work with the management of a theatre, an orchestra or a museum for a period, in order to introduce it to new and improved techniques of organisation, financial control, marketing or whatever the case may be. The experience, if it is still to be considered as that, has proved to be to the advantage of both parties, to the museum or the theatre because it can produce a marked increase in efficiency and to the sponsoring body because it broadens the experience of the person concerned and, by allowing him or her to be observed in a different context, it may reveal characteristics or talents which were not previously obvious.

As this form of sponsorship grows – sponsorship is not really the right word and may already be becoming outdated – it will, inevitably, tighten up the organisation of museums and give them more the flavour of businesses. There are those working in museums who deplore this development, but in general it seems to be welcomed. The real breakthrough, the guarantee of an ultimate revolution in museum planning and administration, in fact came a good deal earlier, with the introduction of computers into museum offices. Once this had happened, and the date has varied enormously, according to the personality and ambitions of the director, the old, easygoing world was dying, if not dead.

This new people-partnership need not, of course, function in only one country. Once it is realised that a museum has a duty to itself and to the public to make sure that its resources, human and material, are used as effectively as possible, that the aim must always be to make one pound of income do the work of two, sponsorship begins to loosen up, and free itself from its paying-for-exhibitions straitjacket. The present sponsorship position is in some ways not unlike relief schemes for Third World countries, eternally piecemeal and effecting no permanent improvement. The more imaginative and progressive sponsors throughout Europe and America have begun to realise that money should breed money and not be regarded as an end in itself. The parallel with the developing countries is fairly close – £100 given to an irrigation project or to road-building is worth much more in the long run than £100 in the form of bags of flour; £100 directed towards providing a reliable water-supply is much more valuable than £100 for a hospital which attempts to cure people once they are ill. For reasons of self-respect alone, museums should be helped and encouraged to earn their own living and provided with the tools to do so. Perpetual grants, whether from private or public sources, are a confession of weakness and possibly failure. Properly managed, museums can be wonderful generators of income, but the ways in which this can be done have as yet been hardly explored. One of the main functions of today's and tomorrow's sponsors is to indicate to museums, by training and practical example, how this can be done. Intelligently handled, 1992 could be of great value in pointing the nose of sponsors in the most productive directions, so that museums, theatres, opera houses and all the other branches of the arts can rid themselves of the begging-bowl complex which has sapped their energy and initiative for so long.

In all such matters, one is talking of co-operative matters and of someone taking a lead. The whole point of 1992 as a symbol is that it implies the beginning of the end of the division of Europe into self-contained national compartments. Not that small units in themselves are necessarily inefficient. One large plumbing firm with a central headquarters and an area of a hundred square miles to cover is almost certainly not as efficient, from the customer's point of view, as fifty plumbers spread over the same area. It is equally doubtful if twenty composers or artists, working as a co-operative, would produce better music or more music than the same number of people looking after their own affairs on their own small premises.

There may however be fields in which it is possible to have too many small sub-units. Are there, for example, too many conservation and restoration workshops within the Community's area? Might the same amount of work be done better and more cheaply by concentrating them and possibly halving their number? Every country in the world, not only those in Europe, admits to having a backlog of conservation work which, even if no more came along, would take at least the rest of this century to complete. This is another way of saying that the task is impossible, that the decay of collections is inevitable and all one can do is to establish more or less arbitrary systems of priorities. The problem is said to be fundamentally one of money, but this is not entirely true. If a billion pounds were to be made available tomorrow, to be applied solely to restoring and conserving objects in Europe's museums, it would not be easy to spend it quickly. The additional skilled staff do not exist.

63

There is nothing wrong with a conservation workshop or studio being small. There is a strong case for keeping some of them local and in close contact with the collections and their staff. But they cannot function without trained people and, in general, museums, whether in Britain or on the Continent, and whatever their size, have not proved successful at training in conservation, unless this is carried out in co-operation with a training institution. There is already an extensive network of conservation training courses throughout Europe. They are, inevitably, of varying quality. Britain has a larger number and wider range of such courses than any country in the European Community. They attract a considerable number of students from abroad. The Institute of Archaeology in London, for instance, has been attracting overseas students in large numbers for many years and the courses in painting conservation at the Courtauld Institute and at Gateshead and Hamilton Kerr are the equal of any in the world. So, too, is the paper conservation course at Camberwell College of Art, while the postgraduate course at Hampton Court Conservation Centre is one of only two such courses in the world, and is much patronised by overseas students. A reasonable task for the European Community would be to help to fund and develop these courses, so that more students from other countries could participate in them, and also perhaps to facilitate a greater exchange of staff and students, including the provision of post-training internships in foreign workshops and studios.

It might also be fruitful for the Community to select a small number of existing workshops within the area under its jurisdiction and to classify these as major centres, both for training purposes and for carrying out conservation projects. It would then provide a large part of the funds to allow the necessary people to be trained and it would impress on both museums and national ministries the duty to employ these people once they had completed their training. It is not beyond the wit of man to devise and administer such a scheme. The Polish Government did so many years ago and its government-sponsored institutions for training craftsmen who are expert in restoring old buildings, furniture, textiles, woodwork and metalwork have not only been a model for the world, but have brought Poland a great deal of much-needed foreign currency from contracts abroad.

No-one pretends that the organisation of such a scheme for the Community's Europe would be an easy or a rapid affair, but a plan leading to it is essential, unless the lament for rotting treasures is to become a permanent feature of our lives. One should not, of course, forget that there are those who have a powerful vested interest to maintain a shortage of experts in the conservation field. The best way of overcoming their objections is probably to pay them very substantial salaries as trainers, but there are other methods.

Meanwhile, there is an undoubted shortage to be dealt with and, largely because of an inadequate information system, reinforced by excessive nationalism, skills are being wasted. There are restorers, often with a personal speciality, who could take on more work and ways ought to be found to make this possible. The first task, obviously, is to locate such people and to compile as comprehensive and reliable as possible a register of them. The Conservation Unit set up by the Museums and Galleries Commission has shown how this can be done and the task now facing us is to discover ways not only of internationalising such a register, but of making sure that it is effectively used.

The slogan for the campaigns which have to be waged in this field is 'Co-operation gets more done cheaper'. It applies to so many aspects of a museum's work. Temporary exhibitions are an excellent case in point. In the United States, what are called 'the nine best science centres' each contribute $50,000 a year to a pool, which exists to finance temporary exhibitions, creating an annual total of $450,000. Each of the nine museums agrees to produce one exhibition every eighteen months and receives $250,000 to finance this. The exhibitions are then sent on tour among the nine members of the co-operative, remaining in one place for two or three months, so that each museum always has one exhibition on display. The exhibitions, on such subjects as *The Physics of Music*, are of extremely high quality, far higher than any individual museum could afford to put on by itself. Transport expenses from museum to museum, which are substantial, are met from the pool created by the difference between the total contribution of $450,000 and the exhibition cost of $250,000 for each museum. The subjects are arranged by discussion between the nine parties.

The whole point of the American scheme is that it produces exhibitions of very high quality and that adequate funds are available, through the pool system, to ensure this. A tentative beginning has been made to establish something similar in Europe, with the proposal for a European Science Museum collaborative. A preliminary meeting was held in January 1989, at La Villette in Paris, as a result of which something to be known as ECSITE (The European Consortium for Science, Industry and Technology Exhibitions) was declared to exist. Little, if anything, has happened since that meeting, which was attended by representatives of museums of very varying sizes and degrees of importance, many of whom were obviously in no position to make an annual contribution of anything like $50,000 to a European pool or even to provide suitable accommodation for the kind of major exhibitions which the Americans now stage. The intention may have been good, but the financial resources for such a venture are simply not there at the moment. Whether the Community can be persuaded to top up what money is available is a matter for conjecture, as is the degree of priority which should be given to it.

The Community has wonderful opportunities to work out a system at least as good as that provided by the Government-backed Riksutställningar in Sweden not only for travelling exhibitions, but for the whole range of museum specialities. The present system, or lack of system, of country-by-country, city-by-city and museum-by-museum exhibitions is ludicrously inefficient and equally ludicrously expensive. It represents a poor use of money. The responsibility of the Community is certainly not to organise exhibitions, but it is reasonable to expect it to provide funds for the operation of an international planning committee which would have this function.

One would hope, too, to discover some way of rationalising the museum studies which are at present carried on under the heading of Research. There are a great many useful things about which Europe's museums need to have up-to-date and reliable information and certainly dozens and possibly hundreds of people are working in universities and research institutes throughout Europe in order to produce papers and theses dealing with these matters. There is, however, virtually no co-ordination between the various projects. Twenty people may, for instance, be researching into the not unimportant matter of museum texts, with research grants to help them on their way, but it is perfectly possible for any or all of them to be unaware of the others' existence. It is always a matter of argument as to whether a piece of research, especially at a university, is primarily for the benefit of the public, of the community of scholars or of the particular individual responsible for it. With so much public money at stake in the museum field, one would hope, however, that some part of what might be called museum-research would be plainly and obviously for the public good and that the overall programme of research might be co-ordinated in some way. Anything resulting from 1992 which led to this would surely be welcome.

The mechanics by which the desirable goals described above could be realised are discussed in the next section of this report.

Meanwhile, it is interesting to observe that one type of development which is taking place with increasing speed and intensity within the Community is most unlikely to be of any direct concern to museums. Cross-border take-over bids for museums are not likely to occur, except in the purely private sector, that is, where no question of public ownership or charitable status is involved. One charity cannot legally take over or absorb another charity, even in another country, so that, say, the National Motor Museum at Beaulieu would find it very difficult and probably impossible to merge with a corresponding organisation in France or Germany, attractive as that might be from a business and perhaps also a cultural point of view.

One feature of the British museum scene, however, could be repeated on the Continent. The Science Museum is now, by any reasonable definition, a museum corporation or, as some might say, empire, with its headquarters in London, in Exhibition Road, and branches in Bradford (The National Museum of Photography, Film and Television), York (The National Railway Museum), Wroughton (its heavy machinery centre), Yeovilton (Concorde) and, in the making, on the Royal Agricultural Society's Showground near Warwick (Agriculture). There is as yet no museum federation like this anywhere else in the world, although the Tate Gallery, with a mother-museum in London and branches in Liverpool and at St Ives, and the National Portrait Gallery, which distributes its collections between London, Bodelwyddan in North Wales and Montacute in Somerset are beginning to tread the same path. There are odd instances of outpost-museums on the Continent, but the practice is very rare, except in Austria, where a group of museums in Steiermark operates as a kind of federation, under the heading of the Joanneum, based in Graz. It would be surprising, however, if, for reasons of efficiency and economy, similar federations did not develop elsewhere in the near future. One is, in fact, already in its initial stages in the Mulhouse area of Alsace.

The fluidity of the situation is well illustrated by what has just happened in Utrecht, at the National Railway Museum. Until 1988, this museum received an annual grant from the Ministry of Culture, to cover all its expenses. The amount was, of course, increasing annually, to compensate for inflation. In 1989, the Minister agreed to exchange this annual grant for a single capital sum, which the Museum is free to invest as it chooses. If it invests wisely, it will do better than before, but if it makes mistakes with its investments, it will do worse. The National Railway Museum was a

State museum. It is now a trust, free to manage its own affairs. Such a situation would have been unthinkable even five years ago. How much capital would the British Government have to find in order to buy out the Science Museum, or for that matter the Science Museum's child, the National Railway Museum in York?

One could perhaps view the 14,000-odd museums within the area of the European Community as a giant laboratory, in which 14,000 experiments are being carried out with varying degrees of energy, imagination and efficiency, to discover the most fruitful and most practicable ways of running a museum. Each of these museums has what it believes are its own peculiar circumstances and problems but, with the help of a computer, these might well reveal significant patterns, patterns of finance, patterns of staffing, patterns of the numbers and types of visitor, patterns of organisation, patterns of success and failure. Such comparative information is not at present available, except in the most piecemeal and unsatisfactory fashion. This has two consequences, both of them bad. The first is that each museum is treated as an island unto itself. Its way of going about its business is not, except incidentally, communicated elsewhere. The second result is that wild generalisations are made all the time, simply because the real facts and the context of those facts are not known outside each museum. Rivalries, prejudices, ignorance and ambitions are not for the computer to identify and evaluate, but the facts at the root of these manifestations are not insuperably difficult to state objectively and perhaps to quantify.

As it is, we are far from well-informed as to what actually goes on in Europe's museums. We know far more about industrial and commercial businesses than about museums. If every museum had to reveal its annual balance-sheet, to take only one aspect of the information we need, a great many people would be very surprised at the picture it presented. Once one knows what income an institution or an individual receives and how it proceeds to spend the money, much that was previously dark becomes clear.

The most important gift that the Community could make to the museums within its bailiwick would be to enable them to have an adequate information system. This forms the principal recommendation in the next section.

Section D
Recommendations

In the present highly nation-based and to that extent anarchic situation, any list of recommendations has to steer a middle path between idealism and realism. The proposals which follow are made with this in mind and in no order of priority.

1. The present system, or lack of system, of applying for Community grants should be greatly simplified and the procedures speeded up.

2. A committee or sub-committee should be set up with Community backing to look at the availability and potential of sponsorship within the area as a whole and to suggest improvements. Such a committee or its officers might accept the responsibility of acting as a clearing house, both for requests and for sources of sponsorship. It is doubtful if existing organisations, such as the Association for Business Sponsorship of the Arts in Britain, would meet the need. They cover too wide a field, in which the tendency of commercial enterprises to concentrate their patronage on prestigious exhibitions is very marked. Something concerned specifically with museums is required.

3. A sub-committee should be established as quickly as possible to investigate the working of VAT, as it affects museums, and to make recommendations.

4. A study should be made, on a European basis, of the present methods of selecting the people who intend to make museum work their career, and to enquire whether a more scientific approach, based on modern selection techniques, might produce better results.

5. The terms 'professional' and 'museum profession' should be used with greater care and discrimination.

6. Much more attention should be paid to in-service training, in order to make sure that it corresponds both in quantity and in quality with the real needs of the people, at all levels, who work in museums. All museum staff should be obliged, as a condition of their employment, to undergo such training.

7. There should be adequate and attractive financial rewards for

those who improve their qualifications as a result of in-service training. Particular incentives should be provided for employees who develop a higher level of proficiency in foreign languages. It is especially important that this should apply to secretarial staff.

8. A detailed and reliable study of European museum salaries should be undertaken.

9. There should be greater increased travel possibilities for museum staff. Ways should be found by which the people directly involved can earn some part of the cost of such travel, regarding this as an investment in themselves.

10. Much more attention should be given to the selection and training of museum administrators. The appointment to administrative posts of people with a non-museum background should be encouraged. The possibility of a European staff college for museum managers should be actively considered.

But the fundamental need, within a European Community which aims to achieve some measure of co-ordination between its museums, is for an adequate information system. Such a system would, as a minimum, be responsible for carrying out the following tasks:

1. The location and recording of all museums within the Community, no matter what their size and form of ownership. This information does not at present exist.

2. The recording of the number and category of the paid employees of each museum, with the name of the director or curator.

3. Obtaining the latest annual budget of each museum.

This information would be continuously up-dated and would constitute the basic store of information about the Community's museums. To it would be added the following records, also regularly revised:

1. The titles and dates of the forthcoming special exhibitions in each museum.

2. Details of lectures, training courses, conferences and seminars to be held in each museum.

3. Facts about any important changes which had recently been made or which were about to be made to the premises, collection or displays of the museum.

4. Details of vacant posts and of the qualifications required for them.

5. Details of experts in particular fields, such as textile conservation and the restoration of historic machinery.

This information would be fully computerised from the beginning, with an appropriate staff to receive and process it. Without it, in an easily accessible form, on-line, by telephone enquiry or in some printed form, co-operation between the Community's museums will continue to be seriously handicapped.

In order to realise such a project, the Information Centre would need a base. This should not be in Brussels, where it would be swamped by other and larger activities competing for attention, and where the bureaucratic atmosphere would militate against the efficiency and friendliness which are essential to its proper working. It should be attached to some place or institution which is already identified with museums, and only museums, in the public and professional mind. It must have a strong identity from the beginning and a name which goes well in all the languages of the Community. The name COMUS, short for The Community's Museums, might do very well.

It could very suitably be located in Britain, possibly in Leicester. English, not French, is the first language of the Community and this fact would be emphasised by establishing such a centre here. The funds required in order to set up and staff such a base would come from the Community's central funds. The staff, from the beginning, would be international and multilingual. They would have to be appropriately paid. Working at COMUS would in itself be an excellent form of training for other posts and should be publicised as such. A high quality of personnel is essential.

The establishment of COMUS would be associated with the development of a system of publications, some of which would be self-financing, or almost so, while others would require a Community subsidy. They would probably include:

1. A monthly bulletin, *News from COMUS*.

2. Sectional computer printouts of, for example, job vacancies and forthcoming events, if it feels better to do this than as part of *News from COMUS*.

COMUS would need to have an active, reliable and respected national representative of each of the Community's member states.

These people would form the COMUS Committee and they would have quarterly meetings in each country on a rotation basis. One of the Committee's duties would be to organise a regular programme of activities involving both professionals and interested members of the public throughout the Community.

COMUS should be seen as very much a British initiative and it should be well publicised as such. Within it, there would be no specifically British interest. Everything in the above outline would be of direct benefit to museum professionals in this country.

There is, however, one task which is of particular British concern which needs to be dealt with very urgently. That is the improvement of the language skills of British museum professionals. If nothing is done about this, museums in Britain are going to find themselves increasingly at a disadvantage. This is of great importance in any scheme which aims to bring Britain and the Continent closer together and to make sure not only that British museums receive their fair share of benefits from 1992, but that they share their many strong points with the Community.

APPENDIX
The Organisation and financing of the Community's Museums

Comparisons between the Community's member states are not easy, partly because ministries carrying the same name do not necessarily have the same function and partly because terminology varies a good deal. The different meanings of 'State museums' and 'National museums' are a particular source of confusion.

Belgium

In museums, as in every other aspect of the national life, the situation is greatly complicated by the existence of two cultures and language communities, the Flemish and the Walloon (French), each of which demands an equal share of prestige and public provision. This is grossly inefficient, but, in the interests of civil peace, inevitable.

Museums are consequently 'communitarised' and the responsibility of two Ministries, the Ministry of National Education (French section) and the Ministry of National Education (Flemish section), but their influence is not always significant, as most museums are run by towns or associations, and their control is, in practice, restricted to the subsidies they provide to museums in their own community.

There are two museums which depend wholly on the Communities, the Musée Royal de Mariemont for the French Community and the Museum of Fine Art (Koninklijk Museum voor Schone Kunsten) for the Flemish. The five Royal Museums are intended to serve both Communities. There is only one genuinely national institution, the Royal Artistic Heritage Institution, which is concerned with research and restoration.

During the past decade, the policy has been to ask certain towns to specialise in their museum provision, in order to avoid unnecessary dispersal of material and overlapping of functions. This policy has had some success. Flanders is now concentrating on modern and contemporary art, Tournai on tapestry, Charleroi on photography and La Louvière on the graphic arts.

Belgian museums lead Europe in making museums or sections of museums meet the special needs of physically and mentally handicapped people. In this, it has had particularly to bear in mind that it has a higher proportion of blind and partially-sighted people than any other European country.

The staffing position in Belgian museums would probably be considered unsatisfactory elsewhere. Only curators in the Royal and Community museums, seven in all, are required to have a university degree and museum experience. The remainder are mostly volunteers and unpaid.

Denmark

Museums in Denmark are mainly the concern of the Ministry of Cultural Affairs, although certain of their activities come within the province of the Ministry of Education and Research. The principal national museums are funded wholly by the State and their employees have the status of civil servants. Most of the other museums are looked after by county or municipal authorities who are able to ask the Ministry for supplementary funds under exceptional circumstances. Their staff, too, have considerable security of tenure. Most of the directors or curators of Danish museums are appointed on the basis of their academic record. There is no system for awarding diplomas in museology, although certain university departments, notably of archaeology and the history of art, include a museology module in their courses and the professional associations organise courses and conferences which give their members an opportunity to widen their experience.

There are three separate museums organisations, one for people who work in natural history museums, one for art museums and one for cultural history museums. Each of these has its own activities and publications. The division has both advantages and disadvantages and has met with considerable criticism in recent years.

Denmark has its own branch of the Association of Scandinavian Museums.

France

Overall responsibility for museums in France belongs to the Ministry of Culture and Communication, whose budget was increased by 40 per cent in 1989. New laws, which came into effect in 1982 and 1983, reduced the degree of centralisation and gave greatly increased power to the regions as administrative and political units. These legal provisions did not, however, affect the division of French museums into two categories, those known as Classified and Controlled (Classés et Contrôlés), which are financed and administered by local authorities or the State, and the rest, belonging to foundations and associations. The second, amounting to nearly half the total, do not officially exist, however important they may be from a cultural point of view.

Career prospects in the public sector of French museums are restricted for those not possessing the diploma of the Ecole du Louvre, which has art history as the core of its studies. Only these graduates are considered for the post of Conservateur de Musée.

There is no professional organisation which speaks for French museums as a whole. Membership of the Association Générale des

Conservateurs de Collections Publiques is open only to those who work, at the Conservateur level, in a Musée Classé et Contrôlé. It has at the moment about 950 members, representing about a third of all those who run museums in France.

Federal Republic of Germany

Museums, like most other cultural activities in West Germany, are the business of the provincial governments (Länder) and not of the Federal government. The only museum in Germany to be financed centrally is the not-yet-opened Historical Museum in Berlin, for which the Parliament in Bonn is finding the money. The State museums, in the sense of National Museums, are in Berlin, financed by the Prussian Cultural Property (Preussicher Kulturbesitz), which took over the assets of the pre-1945 Berlin, when the city was divided.

Rather less than half of all the museums in the Federal Republic belong to municipalities and about the same proportion to associations and foundations. The so-called 'State museums', of which there are many, are misleadingly named, since 'State', in this case, means the old States of Germany, which correspond roughly to the modern Länder. 'Regional' would be a better name.

There is a Ministry of Culture in Bonn and there are Cultural Counsellors, usually excellent, at German embassies throughout the world, but the German Minister of Culture has much more general responsibilities than his opposite number in Paris.

Each of the German Länder has its own museums association and there is a German Museums Association (Deutscher Museumsbund), with its headquarters in Bonn, which brings together regional associations of curators or groups of museums, guarantees the observation of a professional code of practice, and ensures a certain degree of uniformity in the functions and legal status of curators. To obtain the Curatorship of one of the more important museums, it is normally required that a candidate shall possess a doctorate and have had a minimum of two years' practical experience. No German institution as yet awards a diploma in museology comparable to what is available in Britain or France.

Great Britain

The organisation and financing of museums in Britain is peculiar to itself, and difficult to explain to foreigners. Until 1945, there was a basic division between local authority and national museums, the first being financed from local rates and the second from income tax. Since then, the position has become more complicated, with the establishment of a large number of mainly foundation-based museums, the so-called independent museums, which now amount to more than a third of the total.

Britain, as foreigners are not slow to point out, has no Minister of

Culture. In these circumstances the Minister for the Arts has to act as a substitute.

The nearest British equivalent to a Ministry of Culture is the curiously-named Office of Arts and Libraries, which is an independent public body allocating subsidies, not a Government department. Linked to it is the Museums and Galleries Commission, which has 15 members, appointed by the Prime Minister. It advises the Prime Minister on museum matters, provides guidance on conservation services and travelling exhibitions and pays half the cost of the budgets of the Area Museum Councils, the remaining 50 per cent being met by museums within each Council's area. So far, the advisory and grant services of the Area Councils have been available to all museums, but the present policy is to give grants only to those museums which reach certain minimum requirements and qualify for registration. One of these requirements is that there shall be on its staff, or available for advice and consultation, at least one person with appropriate qualifications in museology.

Greece

Greek museums are overwhelmingly museums devoted to art and archaeology. Most of them are small and, with few exceptions, the museographical standard is not high, although charm is widespread. The majority of their curators are unpaid. Museums of science and technology hardly exist, the national natural history museum is a private foundation and there is a handful of folk life museums, mostly privately operated and in two instances excellent. There is no organised system of training and no effective museums association, although there is a Greek National Committee of ICOM.

Responsibility for providing and maintaining a service of museums in Greece lies with the Ministry of Culture and with local authorities, who also share the task of caring for the nation's formidable stock of historic sites and monuments where the standard of written interpretation is generally low, due in part to opposition from the influential and well-organised Association of Greek Guides, an admirable and knowledgeable body, with a well-developed sense of self-preservation.

Ireland

Ireland has about 200 museums, to serve a population of 4 million. With one or two exceptions, they are not among Europe's best. This situation is caused by a shortage of funds, not of enthusiasm. Few great national museums in the world are as inadequately housed as the National Museum in Dublin, although the National Gallery does a great deal better.

The task of overseeing Ireland's museums falls to the Ministry of Education, which has many other claims on its attention and its purse.

The Office of the Taoiseach (Prime Minister) is also involved from time to time. In Ireland, as in Greece, most of the outstanding museums are in private hands.

There is an Irish Museums Association, the headquarters of which was until recently at the Freemasons' Grand Lodge in Dublin. Training courses are concentrated at University College, Dublin, where the experience has been that a high proportion of the successful students emigrate, after failing to find a suitable post in Ireland.

Italy

The balance of Italy's museums is very unusual. According to official sources, there are 740 municipal museums, 724 national museums, 342 private museums and 27 regional museums. Included in the total of 342 for private museums are the country's 257 diocesan museums, which belong to the church and are administered under the authority of their bishops. This means that the number of genuinely private museums is, in fact, very small, 85.

The Ministry of Cultural Heritage and the Environment (Ministerio per i Beni culturali e Ambientali) has total control over the national museums. For each region, he appoints a Superintendent, for each category of the national heritage – architectural, the natural environment, archaeological and artistic and historical monuments. The Superintendents are civil servants, selected by State examination and each of them is automatically the director of every national museum within his region that falls within the area of his competence. All decisions are taken by him and he appoints a curator for each museum, to deal with day-to-day running and professional direction. The curator has no managerial authority.

The Ministry also exercises considerable power over private and municipal museums, through the 1939 Heritage Law, which provides for inspection and control over these institutions. He also advises in the choice of their curators and in practice it would be both difficult and unwise to appoint someone of whom he disapproved.

All museums, except those which are classified as private, are financed from public funds and are forbidden to indulge in any money-making activities, such as running a shop or a café. In addition, all financial bodies which deal with the general public are compelled to give a proportion of their profits, which can be as high as 10 per cent, for cultural purposes, which includes museums.

Candidates for curatorship must possess a doctorate and pass a State or municipal examination. Italy has no form of museological training.

Italy's highly centralised museum system makes what one finds in France seem relatively underdeveloped.

The Association of Italian Museums accepts the professional staff of all types of museum, public and private, as members.

Luxembourg

The Grand Duchy of Luxembourg has fifteen museums. The three most important are in the capital. One, the State Museum of History and Art, is financed directly by the State and the other two, devoted respectively to Natural History and to Art, by the municipality. Within the Cabinet, most of the responsibility for museums falls to the Minister for Justice, Cultural Affairs and the Environment, a complex of interests within which museums are unlikely to have a dominant rôle.

There is no Museums Association as such and none but an ad hoc system of museum training.

Netherlands

The Netherlands is the only European country where the number of private museums, museums run by a foundation or an association, exceeds the number of public museums. Most of the private museums receive help from the municipality, in the form of a grant and/or rent-free premises. Dutch museums, whatever their status, enjoy considerable freedom in their management, decision-making and budgets. The usual system is to have a director, appointed by the governing body, and a curator for professional matters and for the day-to-day running of the museum.

The brief of the Minister of Welfare, Health and Cultural Affairs includes museums. His influence is direct in the case of the State museums, which are the property of the Ministry, and indirect, through the Central Laboratory for the Arts, a national institution whose functions include museological research, conservation and restoration, and the provision of various services to museum administrators.

Hitherto, the only requirement for a museum curatorship has been a university degree. It is likely, however, that qualifications in museology will soon be necessary for candidates. Suitable courses are available at the Reinwardt Akademie in Leiden and at the Universities of Amsterdam and Groningen. The Museums Association (Museumvereniging), a well-run and effective body, also offers courses to its members.

Portugal

The National Heritage (Patrimonio National) has overall responsibility for the well-being of most of Portugal's 250 museums. 13 of these are National Museums, wholly or mainly financed by the State, and most of the remainder are run by municipalities, although a small number belong to foundations and associations. Portugal is one of Europe's poorer countries and neither the Government nor the municipalities have a great deal of money to spend on its museums.

This may in some ways have been a good thing, since there is a lot of museum talent in Portugal and the country has a remarkable number of simple, yet sophisticated small museums, the product of strong artistic sense with little money.

The Ministry of Culture and the Portuguese Museums Association are giving a good deal of attention to in-service training courses and are inviting foreign experts to take part in them.

Spain

The Spanish museums system is to a considerable extent centralised. General supervision is exercised by the Ministry of Culture, within which there are two relevant departments, the Directorate of Fine Arts and Archives (Patronato de Bellas Artes y Archivos) and the National Museums Directorate (Patronato Nacional de Museos). The Ministry is directly responsible for the 21 national museums and for the buildings and acquisitions of the 50 museums whose administration has been transferred to the autonomous regions. The Prado in Madrid has its own special status and budget.

In recent years, the Ministry has followed a very active policy with regard to museums, refurbishing and modernising old-established museums, setting up new museums, providing central services of a high standard and organising in-service training. At present, no universities or other institutes of higher education undertake museological training. Recruitment to the staff of the national museums is by State examination. Curators of State museums are appointed by the Ministry of Culture, and curators of the national museums transferred to the autonomous regions by the cultural advisors of the autonomous regions.

Printed in the United Kingdom for HMSO
Dd 292009   C20   6/90